PETAL PAINTED BLACK
incorporating
PETAL WITHIN A NETTLE

Kate Dobrowolska

Published by Kate Dobrowolska
Publishing partner: Paragon Publishing, Rothersthorpe
First published 2019
© Kate Dobrowolska 2019

Cover artwork: Lewis Sharpe

ISBN 978-1-78222-695-6

Book design, layout and production management by Into Print
www.intoprint.net
01604 832149

Dedicated to:

Hope, Faith and Love

Kate Dobrowolska

My Life
This book is a journey of hope and faith.

Petal Painted Black attempts to explain the gloomy erratic mood swings, which make my moods sexually high and sometimes on the verge of insanity. I suffered an emotionally challenged childhood, unsettled and tormented, which contributed to a mentally disturbed adulthood. I was diagnosed with bipolar disorder in my early 20s. The illness is also known as manic depression. My emotional turmoil started at a very early time of my life. I grew from early infancy having very high sexual feelings, which caused mood imbalance issues in childhood. This autobiography is a raw account of emotions. It contains content of a sexual nature. My illness has a catalogue of different brainwaves that fluctuate and change and drive me mad. There is no shame in stating how you feel, it is best to let out crazy thoughts, it conquers negativity. Life is too beautiful to be marred by black clouds, and I fought hard through the high euphoric mood swings to try and maintain a balanced sane life.

Sadly, I am still fighting the mood swings.

Sigmund Freud, the founder of psychoanalysis, said that *"being entirely honest with oneself is a good exercise"*. My life story is an honest account of my feelings and struggles. I wanted to write my story so that other people with tormented thoughts realise that it's healthy to be outspoken and open. Freud also said:

"Flowers are restful to look at. They have neither emotions nor conflicts".

Sometimes I wish I was a flower because my unstable mind is in a fast-moving confused mess, and my soul withers from disturbed inconsistent brainwaves. I have felt like a wilted flower many times because mental illness has dug in and caused so much personal despair. I have survived the turbulent deranged waves of insanity. I am still surviving. I believe in myself, and I hold faith close to my heart.

Why an Autobiography?

The reason I decided to write about my life is because there are many people worldwide who have a similar illness, and who are suffering through their feelings and cannot put words in a book to tell a story about their struggles. I would like to think that if a person heard about my issues and related to them, hopefully they would seek some comfort in knowing they weren't alone with their feelings. I am lucky that I receive excellent health care, especially when my life became dark in the 1980s, and insanity of mind was prominent, and I suffered lonely years of despair. I am a wife, a mother and sister, but the feeling of being isolated was hurtful within me.

I can coherently write when focused creatively because my mood swings rhyme and flow words. I still have vicious erratic mood spells three times a year, because I suffer Bipolar High, ADHD and Seasonal Disorder, which are affected by light, environment, people, time changes and weather conditions. When I am ill, I have no concept of time, there are no people around me that I am aware of, and I become an obsessed person, in fear of my surroundings and mind-flying on a different level to other people. People think that mentally impaired people are disillusioned, or they are hallucinating but I say I am gifted. I see things with my eyes that other people cannot see, and I hear things with my ears that other people cannot hear. I believe I can sense another dimensional era be it past or future. I am a firm believer in time travelling, and of celestial super beings existing. Fairies, gnomes, goblins and leprechauns have their place in our life, just like angels and mermaids too. Everyone visualises life differently.

These creatures were described in words derived from other people's creative visions. There are millions of books written worldwide, so why would people write these issues?

People write to express themselves, because they have experienced things that they want to share with others. People write because they enjoy being creative, and it keeps them mentally stimulated, and it's a personal legacy left to their family and a historical memory of themselves. People also write to educate, and therefore these are the reasons I have written my autobiography. I hope that whoever reads my written work develops an understanding of mental mood madness, and realises that people who suffer an unbalanced life have an exceptional thought process, an unusual brain, a great intelligence and are gifted as individuals. I am unique, and I'm not alone.

My Background

I was born in Mountsorrel, Leicestershire, to Polish parents. My parents were Polish refugees who could stay in England after World War 2. My mother's birthplace, Lesznow, belonged to Poland, which is now part of Ukraine, because the peace treaty at the end of the Second World War divided countries with new borders. My father came from a place called Galkowek, which is near Lodz. He was in the Polish army but under British army command, and he could stay in England after the war because the Soviets took over Poland, so he couldn't go back. My father became a porter in a hospital after the war ended, where he met my mother who was ravaged by illnesses she caught abroad when she was a displaced refugee living in Bombay, which is now Mumbai.

Mother eventually travelled to England to settle but became hospitalised and very ill. My father, upon meeting my mother, scrutinised her weak, frail appearance and offered to marry her when she felt better, because he said no one else would marry her in her condition. She replied she was dying anyway so he was too late. Well, I am here at 57 years old with two brothers who are in their 60s so we are grateful our mother survived to marry our father. Our parents gave us a chance to live in a country that was liberal and not affected by the communism that oppressed central and eastern Europe at the time. I will always feel gratitude to my late parents for forsaking their homeland to enable me to grow up without persecution. Bless their souls.

I grew up in the 1960s, a wonderful era to develop in; people were friendly, and jobs were plentiful, and life was carefree in my rural village. I suffered minor bullying from ignorant families who didn't understand why Polish immigrants could settle, but in my heart I will always cherish the people I knew and grew with, and I will always have fond memories of my childhood.

My mother wanted to live in the USA because her younger half-sister settled there, but she was too ill to travel that far; fortunately her other half-sister came to England with her, forsaking her chance to settle in USA with her own sister.

My aunt Jozia (Josephine) showed a beautiful loving bond of caring for my mother, even though they were born from a different mother.

My mother's inner spiritual strength helped her cope with several terrible diseases. I am nothing like my mother in personality. My mother was a beautiful soul who never thought badly of anyone or judged people. A quiet, praying lady and caring towards everyone, whether she knew them or not.

The severe mood swings I endure, seem to have been inherited from my father's side of the family.

I have come to terms with knowing I will never feel completely fulfilled as a person and I will always have a challenged life until death.

Bipolar robs people of relationships, makes a mess of their working life, and encourages such severe highs and lows and sadness. I have held down jobs but only short term. I have a formidable character, and I speak truth with more honesty than people can cope with; it is very difficult for me to bite my tongue and have more sensitivity in conversation with others who cross my path. I am a driven woman, and in everything I do I make things grow bigger, so I have missed my vocation in running a successful business. Although, in my heart from a very young age, I felt strong desire to be a missionary and educate children in Africa. Bipolar is soul destroying but I channel my excessive turmoiled energies into a functional way of living when I can, and when I feel well enough to tackle anything in life, I try to give it a hundred percent effort.

Inherited Bipolar

My father suffered traumatic mood swings, a form of post trauma stress. The artillery noises during the war in Poland contributed a mood madness and this nerve-wracked ill health stayed within him when he settled in England. I feel that the turbulent environment I grew up in made me a highly nervous angry child, and I believe that the environment a child is born into does contribute enormously to their character and personality moulding. This is because we all emulate habitual behaviour from people who impact on our lives. This can also play a large part in mental instability, if triggered, as our memory stores all life patterns we think, feel and act upon.

Recently there have been suggestions that bipolar disorder in parents has a link in children who have ADHD, and I agree with this. ADHD does exist, because I have been diagnosed with it, and it is a fast thought process in the brain and it is hard to control, especially when a person has erratic vertical bipolar waves as well. I also feel that OCD will have a similar difficult to control mind wave as one of my sons seems to suffer badly with obsessive cleaning.

I hope this book will be of help to anyone who has poor mental health, or a family member of someone with poor mental health, or a psychology student, a doctor, or a person who wishes to learn more about mood-related illnesses, because I write about my emotions openly and can look outside the box to write all I know from my own troubled thoughts.

Banishing ignorance of people's mental ill health is the key to helping those who suffer with mind issues. I am passionate about contributing my personal knowledge of mental illness through a book, and I hope this book will be well received and encourage other people to write their, or their loved ones' life stories too. There's nothing worse than the dreaded line "Pull yourself together!". It's not easy to do that, it truly isn't; but if issues are raised and understood, it can encourage someone to help someone else, and so encourage that person to help themselves.

So, my life story begins from the very beginning…

Kate Dobrowolska

Journey Born Beginnings

Feelings warming, pulsating heartbeats, cocooned in a bubble of love. Safe, secure, a fighting spirit. Who remembers being in a womb? I do. Yes. I really do remember nestling in my mother's womb. I remember through my feelings. I sense aura, I feel energy waves, I feel environment. I am an unborn empath with sixth sense, and I am tucked up, nestled in a cosy shell waiting to be born. I can hear things in my mother's stomach, I can hear gurgling sounds, rushing sounds, heartbeat sounds, I feel the waves of the amniotic sac every time my mother moves, and I can see mingled shades of grey and darkness. There isn't time span inside my mother's womb, so the environment feels safe and warm … and then – a surge of disruption:

Explosion, disruption, turmoil, gushing energy surges, feelings of descending pulling, greyness and *OUT!*

Out into a grey misty air. Swoop up, swoop down, Hurt! I scream. I scream because I have been turned upside down and slapped to awaken my senses and gulp the air. I am breathing, airwaves pull into my lungs. I am born. I am a unique infant.

Comfort. I can smell a distinctive scent of bonding.

I am cosy. I sense that I belong, there's a soothing aura around me. I see grey shades, outlines of figures. I hear bustle and muffled noises. I feel protected and safe. I am in the arms of my matriarchal guardian. My mother.

The environment is busy. Airwaves feel fast. There's So much confusion. The environment moves fast, like levers of energy pulling in different directions.

Pick me up. Put me down. Roll me over. Change me. Undress me. Arm pulls, leg pulls. Lots of cuddles. Lots of smells. Outlines of many faces and figures.

I learn who is the closest in bloodline. Their aura feels strong. The airwaves pull tighter to my body. My brothers are special. I am close to their auras, the feelings are so intense. The strongest of bondings are in the early infantile baby development. The early childhood beginnings.

Something is missing. I feel an empty space, a vacuum unfulfilled. The missing link explained in my primary years. He was taken away, before I was born, extracted from the womb like a lemon squeezed from the juicer, his limp fleshy lubricated foetal body drained away into a crumpled broken heap: he was aborted.

Mother couldn't cope, she did the unthinkable, she aborted my brother at a time when it wasn't allowed.

It was for the best. The environment at home was unstable, she didn't want the pressure, the worry, the uncertainty, the pain of coping. Mother was a Catholic. Her life must have been stressful to have conceived this act of Catholic sin. My father behaved aggressively, within the home, and Mother sensed it would be difficult to bring up another son, when they already had two beautiful boys.

My patriarchal guardian, my father, was an angry man. He trembled a lot and he seemed constantly agitated. Air was tense in the house when he raised his voice in irritated anger. Father's behaviour was too erratic. I could feel air suffocation from his shouting and volatile airwaves, which made me nervous as a young toddler. I felt immensely irritated at such a young age.

I cried a lot, I was discontent and insecure, but equally, in a strange way, I felt the home was a secure safe environment, and I seemed to understand that Father was an ill man not a dangerous man.

The Polish family home was my special world. Polish language is a beautiful language and within the four walls of our home, traditional Polish upbringing was compulsory. My parents struggled to speak English correctly, and neither sought education to learn English. We lived in a village, five miles from the nearest town, so it was a quieter place to live, for my parents to work and raise the three of us. My father was an intimidating formidable man with a kind generous heart.

Father's actions within the home were far more frightening than his booming voice. He performed such unpredictable motions of unexpected dominance and fearlessness. I could feel his vibrations in the air, his veins bursting out of his arms, his face becoming more ruddy and bright, and ready to explode. This made me flinch and jump, breeding inflamed anger into my blood. I felt an aura of bewilderment, fearfulness, and uncertainty but I never felt unloved, just empty and hollow in my spirit. I felt incomplete as a child and became an idealistic dreamer. My gut gnawed me and made me feel dense and heavy headed, which seemed such a burden to me as a young child when aware of these sensations.

I bore a black cloud hovering over my head, and my veins in my arms pulsated an aggressiveness that seemed unnatural for my pre-school age.

Faces. Many faces entered my personal space. I knew who people were before I learnt their relation to my family line, and their position in my life. I felt the gene vibe so young. I could feel a person's bloodline. It's a pulling magnetic feeling in the air. Family members have a strong magnetic field, and they exuded a nice feeling of well-being around me. Friends of family felt kind, and anyone I wasn't sure about felt fearful until I got to know them better. The nice thing about Polish culture is the friendliness within the extended family branches.

My mother came from a family of ten and my father had four sisters, and a brother who died young. My mother's family were two families as she inherited half siblings when her mother died, and her father re-married and his wife bore more children.

My grandad Jan was one of three brothers, so I was brought up to accept all my relatives as equal aunts and uncles, although many died in the World War 2 horrors before I was born. Some of my uncle soldiers fell at Monte Casino and Berlin, and one of my mum's brothers is buried in France.

I accepted my father's mood disorder as an illness inflicted from the war years, and we were a family line who discussed past issues openly and encouraged children to learn how we were all related in ancestry.

The atmosphere was difficult at times, but Father was a very hard-working man who put all his inner strength to provide for his family and tend our council back garden smallholding of livestock, fruit and vegetables. We kept chickens, rabbits and pigeons, and never went hungry due to my parents' excellent farming experience.

I don't think I fully appreciated my father's long hours of labour to keep me in food and clothes until I bought tomatoes from a shop in Oxfordshire as a married woman of 17 years of age, living away from home.

Father grew all his veg from seed on his window sill in makeshift incubators. This was a plant pot covered in a plastic bag with a rubber band around the pot, sat on a window sill until it germinated. Looking back, it seemed time consuming, but I imagine he received great joy when seedlings sprouted. Father also made his own wines and beer and strong vodka. He was very generous with his home-made produce and gave a lot away to neighbours and visiting friends and family.

This grieved a neighbour who sold her produce from her garden to people, the difference between a Polish person and an English person of that era: selling or giving.

My home-life was difficult, as I never knew what mood Father would be in, day after day. My mother kept herself to herself, quietly bearing Father's manic grievances in silence and prayer.

Relationships today wouldn't put up a silent wall like they did in yesteryear, when you put up and shut up and lay on the bed you made for yourself.

I am fiery, impulsive, manic, overbearing and unpredictable, just like my father. My children have lived through my erratic mood-swings, just like I lived through Father's. One thing in common that came out of this unpredictable parent saga: we all knew we were loved. That's the difference. In the turmoil of a family home, if you know you are loved you put up with anything; if you are not loved, depression descending upon any age can drown you. Love makes the difference between coping with tensions, or never coping. Father made me feel fearful, but it was a very disciplined fearing feeling. I felt acceptance of his actions and protected, even though he made me unhappy.

I constantly felt anxious within the family home, and there were never dull moments in our house. The tension in the air sometimes felt like a knife waiting to stab, unpredictable and uneasy and draining to absorb as a young child, but it was meant to be. I was meant to be born in this unsettled environment amongst brainwaves of strong emotions.

I was blessed with a beautiful language. The Polish tongue the mother language I learnt first. It felt good to listen to. Pleasurable sensations rippled through my body every time I heard it spoken. Polish was the main language spoken within our Polish speaking home. Mother and Father struggled to speak English although they both understood far more than they admitted to. My naïve young ears were constantly exposing themselves to a sexy sound. When I heard Polish, my groin stirred, and I felt warm inside.

The language was sexually stirring for me. My blood heated my body, and my nerves bubbled with tickling rippling waves of excitement. I felt a sense of belonging, I felt different, and within the childhood family home it was a totally different world to the one outside the front doorstep.

Mother taught me Polish nursery rhymes; she told me about the hardship of leaving Poland, a country caught up in a huge battle of World Wars. Lives lost, birthplaces torn apart, families severed, but freedom for my brothers and I gained, born into a safer country: ENGLAND.

Jedzie Pociąg z daleka
the train is coming from far away,

Ani chwili nie czeka
doesn't wait for anyone,

Jak Konductor laskawy
if the conductor is gracious

Zabierze nas do Warszawy
He will take us to Warsaw

The Polish language is a language which is difficult to translate, but the nursery rhyme about this train journey made me feel trapped in a time warp.

I felt I was there on the journey, the rawness of my feelings felt strong emotionally, I felt pressured, so intense. The nursery rhyme echoes train journey nightmares for those who suffered in World War 2 and never returned; when people were evacuated from Poland, no one knew where they were heading too.

I consumed childhood stress seeing a real-life steam train in the distance out of the window in my home, as my mum sang the nursery rhyme. The stories she relived of her own childhood made me feel dark moods of despair, and implanted erratic doomed seeds of future thoughts that stayed in my mind to thrive and for me to survive for the rest of my living years. I feel this might have been the early onset of an erratic mood instability in me, already at four years old. My mother didn't mean to burden me with her own fears, it was a way of expressing her own anxieties and suffocating thoughts and I accept this and love her even more now she's gone, knowing how much she suffered through her own childhood years.

Communism

The politics and oppression of communism in Europe challenged everyone after the atrocious First World War. World War 2 broke out and land owned by my mother's father and her two uncles was stolen, the families told to leave. The Soviets stripped the 'Zak' families' land and took control of everything they owned; if they hadn't taken it the Ukrainians would have. There was nothing to stay for; they had to go. My mother lost half of her siblings in the war years, and was taken out of her birth place Leszniow and the Polish country she loved. I never really learnt a lot about her life story, as I was blessed to have been born in England and didn't want to distress Mother by asking her to relive her childhood thoughts. All I remember is the story she told me of being on a train journey, not knowing where she was going, and she was told stories of death camps by people on the train, but no one on the train knew if they were true.

My grandad Jan, Mother's father, died during travelling. The train was packed with people struggling for air in a small confined space, and they spent several days travelling without fresh water or food. My mum sat on my grandad's covered dead body because it was more comfortable to sit on than the carriage floor.

This appeared disrespectful, and an old woman on the train scolded my mother. My beloved Aunty Frania, (Francis) defended my mother's actions, claiming there was nowhere to sit, and their father was dead anyway, so he would have felt nothing. I am sure my mum sat in prayer, thought and repentance, as her personality was spiritual. Mother had strong faith.

Mother also told me about the food stop during the long journey, heading towards Siberia. The train stopped for nettle soup and a crust of bread. No one on the train had eaten for three days, and mum was last in the queue and the train hooted to leave. Mother grabbed the bread forsaking the soup and nearly missed the train. My Aunty Frania hauled her into the carriage, and as the train pulled away, grandad Jan was discarded by the train tracks without a burial, as were many bodies in the war.

I don't know my father's story, about his early years, or if he had a happy childhood and loving parents. I can only remember seeing a few photographs of my mother's family, and not of Father and his family. There was a photo of my father as a young soldier looking smart in a Polish uniform, in my family home. He looked fresh-faced and naïve.

I remember my mother telling me that unstable minds were genetically hereditary in his side of the family line as one of his sisters wasn't of sound mind. Mental illness was predominant in Father's line, so maybe that's why little was spoken about them. Mental health issues were brushed under the carpet, as no one knew how to deal with them and couldn't afford a psychiatrist.

I feel that my father's line was genetically strong-willed, and they fought their dysfunctional mind waves with great bravery without medication and doctors' care.

I have never heard of anyone murdered by a family member in my parental family lines, perhaps surprising considering how destructive a mood illness can be when a person loses their mind. Our family line souls are inner kind. To be wholesome on the inside is better than what you project on the outside.

People in body form can hide an inner blackened soul by faking sweetness outwardly, but we live on this Earth as human beings to project outwardly our beauty within. However, negativity and ill understandings breed phenomenally, and the human race finds it difficult to be at peace with so many mingled cultures and ethnic backgrounds inhabiting the Earth.

I absorb immense negativity from everyone and the environment. I project an unsavoury personality that only the closest to my heart can cope with because they know I am burdened with mental ill-health issues.

Brotherly Love and Fear

My two elder brothers are special to me, because they taught me everything I needed to know in my pre-school years. They taught me to speak English. The younger brother taught me to walk and to ride a bike and spent a lot of time in my company and I followed him around like a puppy. I love being around my brother, who is adventurous, cheeky and great fun to be with. He teased me when I was a young child, but I adored him for giving me his time. I felt very loved.

The elder brother is the caring protective brother, the clever studious brother. He came to my rescue whenever I was emotionally distraught; he cuddled me, and carried me to bed when I fell asleep as a toddler. One day my brothers were gone. One went to university, the other into the army. I was distraught, left alone to cope with the waves of irritability and discontent from Father. I felt lonely and sad.

I could play outside on the council housing estate street, on my own at four years old. The life in the 1960s, care-free, simple, creative and fun.

The field next door to my house was a haven to play in and a real bonus for all the children who lived near me. We created group clubs of fun and adventure, and I became the leader of our friendship circle.

My mind contained lots of creative ideas in play, my brain moved rapid thoughts. I spoke fast in chat, and I waved my hands about a lot in conversation. I created games for us all to play because I could develop imaginary play easily. We were never bored as children playing together, and we didn't have technological items to distract us. I wasn't bossy, I was stimulating; I wasn't aggressive in speech, I was dominant, but I always felt niggles in my body, my arms, my legs.

I felt aggressive in my growing pains. I was a very moody child. I didn't feel in control of myself, my mind, or body.

I became constantly rebellious in my thoughts and found living life difficult to be pleasing and I still feel that way today. Being bilingual in Polish and English made me feel as if I was split as a person; two people not one. I needed to keep busy, always stimulated, even when alone and the rapid thoughts wouldn't go away.

My life seemed to be running away from me, I never felt right. I felt alone in my own pocket of space. I was one step forward or one step behind everyone else, and I often wondered if anyone else really existed around me. Father and I reacted badly together personality-wise. He was my thunder, and I was his lightning.

I developed a lot of phobias as a child, and the volatile environment contributed to the phobias developing. A fear of spiders, a fear of trains, a fear of balloons popping, or the unexpected. A fear of lightning, a fear of the dark, a fear of witches and a fear of cats. I wasn't happy about life, I felt fearful living it. I loved nature and animals. I loved flowers, birds, the clouds in the sky, and hills. Walks along the canal and scrumping apples.

My unpredictable dominant father educated me with long nature walks too, teaching me different types of trees and bird sounds. He carried me over an army of hopping frogs, as I had a phobia about jumping creatures too. I helped him in the garden picking fruit and veg, and eggs from the chicken coop. Our livestock were chickens and rabbits and pigeons.

I felt I was mother nature, I felt I owned the Earth, I felt like this at such a young age. I always painted a bigger picture in everything I felt and tackled.

From my infancy I felt 'out of control' urges.

I liked fingering myself. My petal was constantly hot, and I loved rubbing it. I needed to expel the young frustrated anxiety and I expelled it regularly; it helped my angry head thoughts to fade. When I didn't do the finger exercises, I felt sullen, moody, erratic, irritated, explosive, and confused. Rubbing on 'petal' was letting off steam, relieving tension and calming my mind. Mother said it was naughty. I had to repent and pray. I kissed Jesus on my rosary beads for forgiveness but didn't know how to relieve my jumbled emotions differently. I felt dangerous if I didn't let off sexual steam. My mind was blackened with heaviness with ill thinking, and nastiness.

Sexual feelings came very early in life. I felt sexual feelings from the moment my mother changed my nappy and washed and powdered my genitals, which I affectionately call *'my petal'*. I was sexually aroused every time my mother spoke to me in Polish. The heat tickled my petal which brewed the veins in my wrist to move warmly, and my heart to beat faster.

Mood swings are connected to sexual emotions. I had strong feelings of sexual awareness since I was a toddler, which became a nightmare as I matured.

I developed a lot of impulsive childhood behaviours, and I know I was a difficult moody child to raise.

Zodiac Birth Sign

My star Zodiac sign is Leo – a strong dominant star sign – and I came into the world at 6.35 in the morning.

I am an early to bed early to rise person. I love the dawn; it's the best time of day to be awake for, to wake up to God opening his heavenly sky and for the sun to rise. My mother told me that when I was born my Aunty Frania ran down the street shouting *"A GIRL!"*; that's why I feel special. My family made me feel special.

I believe in the star signs; I believe in the Chinese New Year calendar too. I strongly feel our lives are mapped out from birth, and if astrology doesn't suit the sceptical thinkers then let them be the masters of their own thoughts, as my life will never cross theirs.

The Primary Years: The Petal Blackens

I started infant school in the Autumn of 1966. An overwhelming feeling of despair consumed me, and my stomach jumped. I could have eaten a thousand grasshoppers the way my belly button bounced about. I used to think my soul was behind my eyes, and I absorbed life through my eyes, pushing feelings out through my hidden soul. I now know that my soul is behind my belly button, as the belly button is the knot of life within a woman's body.

The umbilical cord is developed from the belly button, so if it gave me life support as a baby, it also shelters my soul too. Yes, my soul is in the pit of my stomach, that's why it's good to follow gut feelings.

I entered the school building through gates with blue pointed railings. My heart beating rapidly, stimulating great emotional distress, I thought I entered another world. There seemed a lot of activity I never noticed before. The stretch of the road leading to the school at the bottom of my street suddenly seemed full of people and children I never knew existed.

My mother held my hand, and her friend held my other hand. I was squashed between two mature buxom bonny women, my own personal bodyguards, making it impossible for me to escape. My legs were walking backwards, and my body was pulling forward.

Too late for exit, we were standing in front of the head teacher of the infant school, a short likeable lady with an air of authority.

The head teacher peered from her spectacles and asked for my name.

"Boguslawa Katarzyna Dobrowolska," my mother said in broken English; it was the only question she understood to answer for herself. The Polish friend supported her through interpretation and filling out forms. "I am sorry we cannot accept this forename" the head teacher answered. "It is too hard to pronounce. What is the English equivalent please Mrs Dobrowolska?" Her finger waved the pen around in the air in circular movements as she smiled at me. My mum's friend hesitated before speaking on behalf of my mother:

"Kathleen".

Kathleen Dobrowolska evolved from the head teacher's reluctance to register my Polish forenames. My birth identity diminished before my eyes. I became someone else. I felt destroyed and lost wondering *'Why?'*.

I was placed in a classroom and absorbed into the mist of new faces. I didn't realise there were so many children in the village. I thought there were only 12 of us, the kids I grew up with on my street, who suddenly seemed to have vanished, as they weren't in my class.

My class teacher looked strict and 'aged' with a long pointed nose and grey, wiry, wavy hair; her wrists were skinny and protruding. She was clad in a stretched knitted light blue cardigan... She smelt musty.

I hated the atmosphere of the school, I disliked the

teacher's voice, I didn't want to be there – and so when I heard the bell ring for a break, I walked out of the classroom and ran home.

Mother was busy bustling in the kitchen and humming a song. It was only 11am and Mother liked to prepare dinner early, as produce came from the garden and a lot of preparation needed to be done. Father sometimes killed a chicken, pigeon or rabbit before he went to work, so Mother spent a lot of time in the kitchen stripping feathers or skin to boil the fresh meat.

I entered the kitchen and threw myself at her stained apron, my arms clasped tightly around her cuddly stomach. I was determined not to go back to school. I felt displaced there.

Unfortunately for me, Mother didn't share my sentiments and dragged me back screaming. She was shocked I had made my way home alone, even though we lived on the next street and not too far away. Too bad of Father for housing the family so close to the school.

Escape felt good for my spirit. I was determined to do it again. If need be.

The school teachers realised I wouldn't settle down to learning without someone I knew, and so my close childhood friend (who was in another classroom) sat next to me for three days to help me settle into the school environment. I felt comforted and secure, relieved that my bonded neighbour playmate was sitting with me.

I fitted into the education system quite quickly after the initial shock of early attendance. I enjoyed lessons and absorbed information with gusto. The ability to learn made me feel immensely satisfied, but I sensed a feeling of being an isolated misfit. I wasn't English, I seemed different – and having to live with the name *Kathleen* really unsettled me – and there was only one other girl who bore a foreign-sounding surname in the village school we attended; other children had normal English surnames.

I wasn't popular at school, I was 'interesting'. The more interesting I became, the more the feelings of isolation grew and the more introverted I felt. I became so shy it affected performances in some subjects. Insecurity made me too scared to ask teachers for support. I copied answers off another friend, so when she got something wrong, I did too. The teachers took a great interest in me; I was a breath of fresh air to them and they asked me so many questions about my parents' background. I knew what to tell them as Mother had taught me everything about her background. I learnt World War history earlier in life than anyone else around me.

I really believe I have lived through war years through my mother's genes. I believe I was there during Mother's troubled war times – just as if I were a time child.

Going to school helped to relieve the tensions back home. Father got progressively worse in his attitude, his behaviour, his volatile outbursts. When I brought friends home to play, we were all nervous when Father came home. I used to disappear into the bedroom when entering the house until I realised Father was having a good day. I'd wait upstairs until Mother called me down for tea.

I felt happier in my bedroom. I felt I could chill and relax and fantasise and switch off from the pressures of living and breathing. I could play with my petal too; it helped to cool bad head days to fumble and feel my innocent virginal crack under the covers. I felt stressed by life; people were too much to cope with. I always looked nervously towards the door in case Mother came up the stairs. It was a drag to pile through the prayers on the rosary beads if she caught me acting in sin. I needed sexual stimulation; my head was full of very condensed heavy ill-thinking filled thoughts if I didn't express my sexual needs externally. Sometimes I felt that evil was residing behind my right ear, telling me to behave erratically and badly. Sexual intimacy was not a bad thing for me to think, but thoughts of death and killing were wrong and I held these evil thoughts in my head with guilt. I particularly liked the idea of hurting animals when in a killing frame of mind, but I really cared deeply for animals and nature. Deep inside my soul I knew I had to suppress killing thoughts. Squash them, stamp on them. Rub petal harder to make killing thoughts go away, and it will ease the pressure of the sexual waves and urges that screwed my mind up.

Everything got on Father's nerves. If I spilt my drink on the table, he would lurch out of his chair clenching his fists, then sit down again sweating.

I always felt a stab in my belly when this happened. The unexpected lurches and the threat of unbuckling his belt on his trousers to spank me made me jumpy too.

Father only spanked me with the belt once, for spitting on Mother. He hit me across my bare buttocks hard with the belt; Mother pleaded with him to stop.

I deserved it. No one should spit on their mothers.

It's the way he caught me to spank me I will always remember. I ran into the toilet to escape his rage. I instantly panicked after spitting on Mother. I locked myself in the toilet, I was prepared to stay there for days when death beckoned. *My* death at *his* hands, this is what I thought. Father came to the toilet door and spoke softly to me. It reminded me of the tale of Red

Riding Hood when the big bad wolf talks to her in grandma's voice. Father spoke the same. "Come out my darling daughter, I won't hurt you" he said softly through the door. Just like a naïve young foolish child, I opened the toilet door slowly. Father swung the door wider, grabbed me by my clothes and flung me on his knee. No matter how much I screamed he just belted me harder until my gentle, mild-mannered mother managed to persuade him to stop.

The more irritated Father became as time moved on, the more temperamental and irritated I became also; the arguing between us cut into my soul like a dagger embedding deeply. I loved Father so much, but we just didn't get on. I missed my brothers a lot, but they hardly came home. I felt I was an only child. I did ask Mother if I could have another little brother and sister for company, but she said no. I was enough to bring up. I suffered the bad vibes at home alone. Confused and mind bitten.

Close Relatives

My closest relatives were Aunty Frania and Uncle; they lived in a second floor flat on the next street. They were my second parents. Aunty Frania was Mother's older sister. I sometimes felt I looked more like my aunty than my mother and inherited my aunty's feisty nature. Aunty had a lot of get up and go. She always kept busy.

Aunty was totally different in looks and personality to Mother. She always looked beautiful to me and Mother looked dowdy. I learnt that Aunty couldn't have children. She had twisted tubes, so no babies came out. Babies came out of tubes? How bizarre! Babies lived in tubes in a female body? I knew different. I was there. I remembered life in the womb.

Babies didn't live in tubes. I used to think a lot about why I came into existence. There are so many people in the world and I always felt we were one big family on Earth, we were all connected to each other, as God's children.

We are born to be functional and help each other.

Aunty looked wild and exciting to me. She wore bright red lipstick and heavily made up her face with beige face powder. She wore fox-collared coats. The fox's head draped round one end of her neck and the tail round the other. I feared the fox, it had beady eyes and a stiff pointed nose, and I thought it would jump off her neck, but it never did. She wore a belt with an ivory buckle. I owned the fox collar and ivory belt later in life for a long while, but they got lost in my travels in the end, which makes me sad – to lose personal possessions of my aunt and her memories through my neglect and unsettled adult life.

Aunty smoked heavily, drank socially with a happy spirit, and often suffered great migraines and swallowed tablets to make her head feel better. She used to curse the ammonia in the black hair dyes she used. It smelt strong whenever she dyed her hair, but she always dyed it; I never saw Aunty grey haired.

I didn't understand that Aunty had more money because she didn't have her own children, I just wondered why Mother didn't make more effort to look smart. I felt closer genetically to Aunty; her aura was hot, she had a yellow aura around her.

I saw and felt its glow when I cuddled her.

Aunty and I went to jumble sales regularly at the local scout hut. Aunty used to buy many clothes and make heavy parcels which she would send to Poland, to help the relatives who were suffering under oppressive communism.

Aunty struggled to take the parcels to the Post Office.

I learnt that Uncle had a family in Poland whom he never

saw again. Aunty helped to support that family too, as well as supporting me. I found out later in life how unkind the family lines were in Poland.

They seemed to be fussy with things they received, and certainly not grateful. They complained that clothes were old, and that Aunty sent rubbish abroad. I am sure the relatives in Poland thought that England was paved with money, and yet we were a struggling family. My parents and aunt were factory workers, not academic scholars, and considering how simply we lived our lives, Polish relatives abroad should have been grateful for any support, particularly when my Aunty used to beg doctors for out-of-date medicines to hide amongst the clothes sent to Poland. From a young age I made a mental note: if I was blessed to visit Poland, I wouldn't visit family, I would visit the country. I started to dislike the country of my parents' origin. I felt strongly they were a money-grabbing selfish race of people.

I visited Poland in August 2011. I went to Krakow and Zakopane courtesy of my brothers who bought the holiday as my gift and went with me. Apart from my children's births and my grandson, who is the cherub of my eye, this is my happiest memory.

I am a mother of five – blessed with three sons and two daughters – by two relationships. I feel closer genetically to my sons, but I know I feel this way as I have excessive progesterone in my body, and I sometimes wonder if I absorbed my aborted brother's deposits from the womb when I occupied it after him. I believe that I am a woman with an inner man within me. I believe that the failed relationships in my life were a consequence not only of my mental ill health but also of my idolisation of the men in my family line – no one I have met could ever match up to them.

I will die knowing I never found happiness with a partner, so we cannot have it all can we?

Aunty Frania

Aunty Frania became my idol. I put her on a very high pedestal. She was a wonderful, generous, hard-working person. My spirit. My life. My adopted mother. I loved Aunty very much and liked sleeping over in her home.

Aunty worked in a factory. I don't remember Uncle working; he was always at home. He said he was ill, but he never seemed ill when I saw him. Aunty did everything. She cooked, she cleaned, she did the gardening, she worked. Uncle sat watching television, played Polish music on a gramophone, played cards or prayed, and wrote poetry.

Uncle had a creepy air around him. He had a monkey-looking face that nightmares were made of. When he grasped a cuddle I wanted to escape; everyone felt the same way about Uncle – my cousins, my friends, no one wanted to be trapped in his cuddle lair. He was a shifty man, and a grey aura shrouded him. He always seemed miserable too, and a hypochondriac.

I liked being at Aunty and Uncle's house. Although Uncle gave me the creeps, he was a calm man, and Aunty's house was a quiet sanctuary compared to mine.

Aunty and Uncle made time for me. Uncle taught me card games and helped to improve my reading and writing in Polish, and Aunty taught me to sew. I learnt to use a pedal sewing machine when I was very young. I made clothes for dollies and teddies and stuffed toys from patterns and materials. I made a stuffed toy gift for a visiting cousin; 'angel' cousin treasured my gift for many years.

Aunty bought me new books every week. I became obsessed with Enid Blyton; the style of her writing absorbed me. I felt connected to her books and I read two sides to the stories. I thought there were reading codes between the lines to crack and decipher.

Enid Blyton seemed a two-faced person and appeared to belittle people in stories. I thirsted for books; I read them fast – Aunty couldn't keep up with the demand – and when I was in-between book reading I got black mood spells, heavy dense clouds sitting on my head. Whenever I held a brand-new book in my hand, my face lit up in satisfaction. I loved collecting them in series and sets. I read two or three new books a week, and in-between I went to my local library too.

When I looked at words, my hand sent tingling sensations to the tips of my fingers. I was turned on by a new book! Crazy me.

Lots of things sent my petal into a quiver at primary age. My mind fluctuated a lot, and I became aroused by all sorts of things: scissors cutting paper, the rustle of a chocolate being unwrapped, people drawing or doodling. Writing stimulated my petal bud too. I was born to be sexual over pen and paper. I didn't do much with this feeling of arousal, I just stayed tingling until I slipped under the covers of my cosy bed and had a play before sleep. I constantly needed to let off sexual steam, it was an ongoing orgasmic engine inside me.

I often had recurring fantasies in my sleep. I fantasised about being the queen of men. I fantasised a lot about soldiers too and being their 'darling'. This fantasy heightened when I watched soldier films with Father. I repeatedly dreamt of becoming trapped in a prison with men. There wasn't any sexual action in my dreams. I was just adored and put on a pedestal by soldiers, but the thought of being adored turned my body on and the tingling consumed my petal with a burning desire.

Petal blushed deep red and wet without even being touched in my deep headed fantasy land.

A sexually escalating turning point in my life was the relationship I had with Uncle. A fun cuddle turned into a sexual cuddle and I was only five years old at the time. I didn't feel uncomfortable when Uncle slipped his lips across mine in a tickle and cuddle moment. A full-on mouth kiss turned into a full-on mouth snog. I had no idea what was happening; I just knew I liked the feel of it. Uncle would try and snog me at every opportunity, and the feeling felt nice. I synchronised the snog with a guided rhythmic movement on his clothed crotch. He encouraged badness from me when I was too young to understand. This happened for a year. Uncle groomed my mind to enjoy pleasures with him.

A year later, the passionate kisses turned into a light feel on my petal through my clothes and then another year progressed to Uncle slipping his hand down my pants. I enjoyed this too, but I questioned Uncle's motives as I knew Mother had told me that playing with petal would make my fingers drop off.

Uncle told me not to worry, that he played with my mother and aunty's too and they both enjoyed it and so I thought it was ok. I never talked about it and it saved my fingers from doing it to myself. Uncle oiled my petal well but sadly he caused a turbulent wave of aggressive emotions to fester by the time I was ten years old. The aggressiveness and moodiness turned into very bad verbal swearing, and I wore out my mother's patience to such an extent that she threatened to put me into a children's home. Members of my family just thought

I was a very spoilt child. It was bad enough for Mother to have to endure my father's aggressiveness, let alone my moods becoming nastier.

Uncle's sexual intimacy with me was a great sin. My irritable moods became more intense and troubled my mind to a confused oblivious turmoil. Uncle was responsible for muddling my moods further. The more he meddled with my petal, the crazier my mind felt. My relationship with Father deteriorated further; I was starting to give Father very bad heart pains through all the tension and character clashes between us. I constantly felt a sheet of invisible glass between us. We bounced off each other with emotional ego bruising.

I reached ten years old and was wiser in sexual awareness from chatting with children at school. I told Uncle to stop his attention, and from that moment Uncle changed his attitude towards me and started to dislike me. If Father had found out the reasons why I became more aggressive, I knew that he would have fought with Uncle, as they always had disagreements and had never liked each other. I am glad that Mother and Father and Aunty never knew about the intimacy.

Eventually Uncle passed on. I could bury him and his perverse character forever and rest my soul.

Prayer and Worship

Religion, church and worship were a large part of my growing years. My mother practised as a strict Catholic. I had to pray every morning and night and say the prayers out loud. Mother Mary was a huge icon in our home, and Jesus too, but I always preferred to pray directly to God. I believed in cutting out the middle man and aiming for the top boss. This attitude did not go down well with our Polish priest. My first confession before my Holy Communion ceremony lasted no more than 30 seconds. My mother was mortified when I scurried out of the confessional box announcing that I only confessed my sins to God not the priest, because I believed a priest was as much a sinner as anyone else. Mother apologised profusely to the priest and pushed me in the confessional box again, whispering in my ear to make it last a few more minutes. I reluctantly did so, but confessed waffle, like swearing at my friends and getting angry with people, all the time wondering what a big deal confession seemed to be.

I rejected my Catholic faith at the age of 14. I think this teenage time is a turning point in many young people's lives for all sorts of reasons.

I was tired of the monotonous deathly songs and the boring sermons and decided that a chat to God alone was the best way. The spiritual unknown unseen force was far bigger than Mary or Jesus. Father wasn't pleased when I stood up to him and refused to go church. I argued that he never went to church except for key ceremonial events, so why should I? He replied that he was a Baptist, so it was the wrong church.

I had no idea who Baptists were at the time, such was the ignorance of other Christian denominations in the 1970s. I believed Father's reason and never mentioned church again. I became rebellious and turned my back on the Catholic church and I prayed to God personally by chatting.

Faith was in my heart, and I had a direct link to the *'he'* almighty unknown energy force.

Mother and Uncle were always in competition with each other when it came to daily prayers with the rosary beads. Mother seemed true, loyal and pure in prayer. Uncle painted my petal with black tinges, so I saw him as false in prayer. He made me feel sick every time he chanted prayers at home. He said that Pope John Paul II was his best friend; he said he had known him in Poland.

I didn't care what Uncle said or thought; he turned me into an aggravated monster child, and I lost any love I felt for him, forever.

I felt very passionate about things in life.

I loved my village of birth, I loved my local town, my county and my country of birth. Father and I continued to bicker, and he made me feel confused. I was born in England, but he expected me to be patriotic to Poland. I never visited Poland as a child, and as much as I spoke Polish at home and had Polish speaking family around me, I was left utterly confused about the significance of supporting a country I never visited.

I suffered a terrible identity crisis as to whether I was Polish or English and this just added strain to my turbulent mood head. I developed another fantasy…

I wanted to be able to hear everyone's language run through my ears and understand everyone's foreign tongue. I wanted to be the world leader of peace for all nations. These thoughts made me feel powerful and important for humanity, and I believed in my own fantasies as a mind troubled teenager.

Child Abuse

I believe that England takes child abuse too lightly. A child who trusts in an adult trusts the love from that adult to be safe. The mind torments from a young body meddled with; it is terrible for the victim. An adult is wrong to stir the emotions of a child; this stirring causes confusion, irritation, moodiness and violation.

Many child abuse court sentences are too lenient, and the

protection of children is very poor unless there are numbers of children involved and therefore more witnesses to put forward. Fortunately for child abuse victims, cases can remain open for years and the abuser can still be found to be guilty and convicted later in life if there is enough evidence.

However, this is at a cost to mental well-being, and results in children growing up suffering deep depression with the memory of their violated childhood for many years; it contributes to a future blighted by mental illness if the past festers and is not forgotten.

Mental illness is a profound illness that develops in all sorts of people whatever their background, and it is seriously underestimated and dealt with poorly in many parts of the world. Physical and mental pain to anyone is bad but to the vulnerable, like children and the elderly, it is wicked.

I felt the confusions of my childhood grow worse because I was meddled with by Uncle. It is hard to tell a parent if a member of the family is being a disgrace, especially when the abuser family member financially supported the growing years of a child. I wish I had told my parents what Uncle did to me, but somehow I feel that it would have caused a huge rift within the family.

I loved my Aunty Frania so much I couldn't have hurt her heart, and so I suffered – like thousands of children do – in silence and isolation, with severe black moods regularly storming my head.

Animal Abuse

There is no excuse for animal abuse either. Throughout my growing up I favoured animals over people. People made me feel ill. I didn't like being amongst people. I was verbally and physically bullied by some children in my village of birth. This, coupled with Uncle's abuse, made me feel ill-tempered, and I took it out on the animals we owned because there was no one else to buffer my anger. This wasn't my personality in my heart as I always felt great remorse and I never bullied any animal to cause damage physically. Looking back on it I know that I caused an animal mental distress. Some people believe that animals don't suffer mentally, but they do.

I feel animals' emotions deeply, so I used to cuddle them after my angry outbursts. I couldn't handle my emotions from the age of 5 to 16, I felt great waves of mind discontent and out of control brainwaves, and in the 1960s and 1970s there was no Google search engine to explore mental emotions or physical illnesses, and doctors' surgeries seemed to have limited support. Psychiatry wasn't an option for young children or teenagers, so mental illness infested deeper and resulted in angry frustrations from myself.

Thankfully, when I reached adulthood, I eventually became diagnosed with Bipolar 1 disorder, and gaining employment working with animals in a shop helped me to become more loving and caring towards them. I outgrew the animal torments by the time I turned 16. I favour animals over humans now and I find it hard work to be close to my children, family and friends. I do cry over sad situations when humans suffer but I will always feel as if I walk alone as I don't feel as if I belong to this Earth I was born into.

I find it difficult to hold a newborn baby and I usually observe a baby from a distance, rather than cuddle the child. I feel as if I shouldn't impose on a child, because I don't want them to feel my tensions. I have given birth to five children and feel that none of them received enough warmth from my cuddles. I have created a barrier around myself, and I think that all my children have created a barrier around themselves too in my company.

Life does shape us all as we grow and evolve, and as we face challenges that cross our paths daily. Everyone changes their thought patterns and emotions daily to suit the hurdles they cross, but no one realises they make those changes themselves.

Raising 'feel good' positive vibrations creates a happy mind. This doesn't work for a lot of empath-gifted people as other people's negative energies are absorbed like a sponge, and illnesses are born to those who are sensitive to negativity, deceit, dishonesty and lies. I am a recluse and that is how I like to be unless I lower my barrier and welcome a new person into my life. I am a creature of basic habits, and I'm not keen on changing my life pattern, as I feel safer in the cocoon I hide in to protect myself in my illness.

Narcissism and the Soul

I have narcissistic tendencies, as I am obsessed with my eyes, and I can be aggressive within my mind turmoil. My eyes are green and soulful and yet I feel so soulless as a person at times. I often wonder how everyone else in the world feels about their shell of a body and what they see with their eyes. I would love to live through other people's eyes just to see how their perspective appears in vision. My soul has a rebel streak, I am a wild one, and when I became a teenager, I began to feel that my mood disorders as a child were a growing virus, a leech, a nuisance and an ongoing catastrophe. My mind thoughts were dark and deep as a child, and horror films scared me. I even felt ill over negative news on the television. These days I absorb issues in the media with a deep sadness and my outer thoughts are fraught with bitterness at times, because I am disappointed with people and how the world has evolved.

I look at my eyes several times a day, it makes me feel reassured I am ok. I don't feel in my heart I am vain, I have too many body imperfections to be vain. I have developed feelings of anxiety and have a great dislike of being sociable with others. I live life for myself and rarely mix with other people. I don't mean to be aggressive in my personality, but I don't know how to be assertive either and I quite often feel I am the black sheep of the family. The odd one.

People see narcissism as inflicting ill health on others' well-being, but people don't see the clashes of narcissistic people with others in society and the environment. Narcissism to me is a way of fighting back those who look down on me, and those who ridicule me and those who don't support me. I feel as if I am made to stand on my own and the support of my relatives isn't fruitful enough, considering my ill health.

In the past, everyone in my family line viewed me as a difficult, temperamental, spoilt child, but I was a sad child, lonely in a world full of horrible people.

I felt suffocated with the evils that were portrayed on television and in the media; and the segregation of people's cultures; and religions that were ill received. There were a lot of racial barriers, a lot of misunderstanding and ignorance, and very little care support for those not feeling happy. Narcissism is a personality condition in which the sufferer – narcissist – is affected by what he or she perceives in society and in the environment, just like a sociopath or psychopath.

I am not endorsing these personality disorders but when they weren't understood in the 1970s and the 1980s, they weren't treated efficiently either.

I think my obsession with constantly looking in a mirror is also my reassurance that I will be ok; I will survive, because my eyes are kind and soulful, and not evil.

Repetitive checking of the windows of my soul became a ritual habit in the past, that also seemed to be rude to others. I used to whip out the mirror without a thought, even during a church service. This action caused a constant reassurance that I would survive the erratic brainwaves.

I have survived, so far, and I know I have a good soul with a complicated outlook. My soul is pure. I am here to view and absorb the Earth's issues until I leave this Earth to travel to a higher plane.

Psychic

Mother told me a lot of things as a young child, things that I now look back on and wonder how she could have known back in the 1960s. She told me that technology would spring forward so fast that people would lose control over it. They wouldn't know how to handle it, and that it would be easy to destroy the world at a push of a button. She said that children would stop playing naturally together, that they would become isolated and obsessed with technological items. She told me there would be a World War 3, but a war of individual minds, not another World War of mass physical destruction with bombing by planes or sea warfare.

My mother said the next world war would be wars inland imposed on individual countries. People would become mind crazy and individually attack others. She told me to keep my mind strong and powerful, and not let the world upset me. She said life would evolve better if people's minds were pure in goodness and strongly united in prayer and good deeds. I had no idea what she meant by all this – I was only four years old – but it was great bedtime storytelling. The power of praying felt important to save humanity, and that's why Mother constantly prayed daily with her rosary beads.

I prayed out loud each day, which I hated as I preferred to talk to God normally and not to chant the prayer book. I reluctantly repeated prayers to please Mother and kissed the Virgin Mary photo before sleep. A ritual I upheld for 14 years until my views on religion changed.

My father told me he preferred another Christian denomination, so I explored the Methodist Church and the Baptist Church and preferred them to the oppressive Catholic one I grew up in.

I have written a poem that comes from my soul. I don't know why I wrote this poem, but I was meant to write this.

Pure Soul Reigns

I write these words from my soul you see,
they flow out fast without a thought,
my thought rhythm has increased in speed,
I write, what I know from within me.
Mothers were cursed, from Lilith and Eve,
The mothers of past fell into three lines,
the inside as black but outside that shines,
and inside as white but outer black clouds form,
and those that were lucky to be happily born.
Every family line has genes that are torn,
people were mixed up until things changed,
a new order is formed, and victory has gained.

The mothers whose soul is as white as snow,
have ascended from heaven and now rule the show,
the mothers of black who claim to be nice,
are not made from sugar but of real hard ice.
Those that are lucky to have grown from the two
are special light workers if only most knew.
The separation in the heavens and the
re-enlightenment on earth, will now
suffocate the badness in time you know,
natural death causes will happen faster, you see,
and the badness of woman will diminish one day,
as the black soul lines will all fade away.

Shine love and light from within your soul today.

Intuition

I have sensed things in my life. I sensed my Aunty Frania's death in 1973, when I woke up screaming in the night that Aunty was dying. Mother rushed into my bedroom and said I was having a nightmare, and to go back to sleep. Dawn broke. I awoke to my uncle shouting hysterically up the stairs that he had found Aunty dead in bed. He had woken early to make Aunty a cup of tea before she rose to go to work, but she never awoke at 5.35am. I was gutted. I screamed out to my mother around 5.30am – the time of Aunty's terminal slumber.

Aunty told me three days before her death that she felt ill in her left arm veins. She was going to let me meet her at the factory she worked in that week as it was a school holiday, but she forewarned me that it might never happen. How could she have sensed her body dying?

When Aunty was dying, I felt my body getting heavier and denser, my breathing becoming shallower. I felt great arm pains in my left arm and my heart started to hurt. Airwaves rippled outside my body, and I felt hot. Then I shivered and became numb, and my mind just knew. That a person had gone.

Aunty's death tore my heart, but an unexpected phenomenon happened to me, when Aunty came to my bed a couple of days later as a vision to say goodbye. No words, no sound, just a face and a body shrouded with a white mist; then gone.

My last memory of Aunty alive was three days before her death. I visited her for tea – she made me goulash and rice – and as I kissed her goodbye outside the front of her flat, she picked a large white-petalled flower from the front garden and told me to take off a petal one at a time, saying whether I loved her or not after each petal. I did it carefully and slowly as I headed home and as I neared my gate the last petal said I loved my aunty. Which gave me complete satisfaction. Three days later Aunty fell asleep permanently. Devastation for my spirit. I was a broken child. Life was sad for me for many years to come.

Father shed tears openly over Aunty. The second time I had seen him weep. The first was over a letter from Poland telling me that my grandad Dziadek had died. After settling in England with my mother, Father never saw his own father again. Grief was deep for him to lose his own father and my aunt. It humbled me. My father really was humanitarian within his erratic spirit.

I just wished we hadn't opposing pressured crazy airwaves between us. My mother and father sacrificed their right to visit Poland, so my brothers and I could grow up in a better life in England. So selfless of them. God bless their souls and Aunty's too; they were taken too soon when I still needed them.

Sensing Aunty's death kicked off a sixth sense of perception I never knew I had. I felt other people's deaths too. I felt gut reactions to people's faces, and a deep inner gut feeling with people I didn't know. I would watch the television and sense some people in the media were coming to the end of their lives. I also sensed other people's deaths. My father's, my uncle's, my husband's grandmother, but I didn't sense my own mother's. Mother's death was a complete shock, but I wasn't in the area when she died, I was in another county enjoying an outing with my husband and sons. So maybe God was kind to spare me intuition grief in that sad time.

I didn't realise that the empathetic feelings I felt were a gift. I thought I was weird and strange and the only person in the world with such thoughts. I decided to close my mind to the weird feelings, as I was scared I would kill everyone off in my family line prematurely, and I am convinced that when I suppressed my mind it brought out a deep psychosis problem that I have struggled with to this present day.

Empaths

What do empaths feel? Empaths have a deep sensitive perception of feeling. Empaths absorb life's problems with emotional feeling far greater than a normal person. Empaths feel weak with exhaustion around negativity. Empaths sense other people's health problems and emulate these problems in the same manner. When my father was dying, I felt his pained heart, I knew he couldn't breathe easily, I felt I too was fading away.

Empaths also develop different forms of psychic abilities because their senses enhance, and they can feel a higher dimension to others; they can read people's emotions and instantly know a liar, and can recognise deceit and dishonesty. However, they don't discuss it for fear of being ridiculed. Empaths are an easy target to be manipulated or even sedated if family members think they are losing their mind.

Empaths believe that people around them – including their own family members – are toxic, and the way society progresses and evolves suffocates them too. Many empaths, including myself, never find the true twin flame or soulmate they belong with. I thought I had, but what I actually found was the opposite to myself.

We clashed badly as a couple and the relationship lasted barely two years. Empaths are special humans, who have a designated role in this world. However, many don't find the reason why they were born special.

I was born to try and fix people with broken wings. This hasn't worked, as people can only fix themselves and that's why I have been challenged with a path of many wrong turns and have become lost in the maze of the matrix system we must conform to. I have been through many failed relationships, but I will never regret anyone I have met.

I believe everyone who has entered my life, was meant to be, and I feel blessed to have experienced so many things and met so many different people in lots of different circumstances.

Some people pass through our life, some stay with us for a lifetime, and some we may never meet because our lives have crossed at the wrong time. We are all meant to be, whatever life patterns we create. I have written another poem, *Love is unkind*. This poem depicts a torn relationship, where another person is involved, and echoes the traumas involved within a triangle.

(Echoes of a torn relationship)

Love is Unkind

How can you think that I wouldn't stay
when I've lavished you with love, in so many ways?
You felt the warmth of my soul dig deep,
the kisses and caresses were meaningful treats.
The happiness in my eyes were lit with care,
when yours were rotting through 'other visions' out there.
They say love is blind it's true, so true,
because evil is the curtain that closed the door for me, and you!
It is easy to turn troubles on the other foot,
when one is hiding a love that's rot.
The apple core turns a brown sour smell,
and while you feed off the decay you will burn 'Hell'.
However, my love, I will always stay true.
I will stand from a distance and yearn for you.
The joy we once shared, may one day return,
if the SHE-DEVIL who's part of your muddled life,
is tied to thick stems of thorns and left there indeed,
and if you don't sever the chains of hungering stupor desire,
You will never regain that feeling of 'hot loved heat'
The flames of a warm woman to help you reach
passionately higher,
then you let drinking encourage you to be
a hay-wired liar,
soured head rhythm wreaks from a soiled mind-pit of despair,
of perverse wanting dreams and needs impaired.
This makes my heart weep who loved you so deep,
so blind so stung, who didn't expect things to go wrong,
When once love was steadfast and oh so strong!
*and the **DEVIL WOMAN'S** grip is binding and tight,*

as much as you try, the witch of the night,
has grasped your pride and chained you to her poison,
through her own loneliness and ugly self-vision, and you weakened to
her soul that's a masked apparition.
The need for greed is inbuilt indeed,
and you both hang on to the chains of lust,
through the dirty waters of devilish must.
My soul weeps as turmoil blows dust on my heart,
that doesn't trust anymore, this has happened before,
life's patterns repeat when a person moves on,
the saddest part is feeling a shredded soul worn.
If you live in the footsteps of the past,
no matter how small, they will return and trespass,
you will never fly your heart in freedom,
if you hanker after smut, you will stay stained and cursed,
by the woman who's chained you to her future purse.
Please sleep on this and realise your sin,
then say a prayer for the one you have binned,
you condemned the person who loved your heart for 'free',
who was there for you, cared for you,
and was meant for you, and now sadly my love, it will never be,
the passionate hot woman has moved on,
and now you mean nothing to me.

You mean nothing to me!

Teenage Years

Throughout my teenage years I suffered erratic vertical head swings, but I didn't realise what was happening to me. I couldn't understand why the moods kept changing. One day I was kind and helpful and pleasant to know, the next day I felt sullen and niggly and my head seemed dense.

I used to take it out on the rabbits and the cats I owned, throwing them in the air and letting them land with a frightened thud. An enormous guilt would overcome me, and I cuddled and stroked the tormented animals until their rapid heartbeats calmed down. I became an isolated recluse, I never made the effort to socially mix much out of school, or join children circles in school break times, choosing to sit on my own and watch everyone chatting and running around.

My head exploded lots of fantasy thoughts, and this contributed to poor memory and I found It difficult to retain studying information in school work or even listen to the lessons properly.

A couple of incidents happened in my teenage years which I feel triggered a further imbalance in my unsettled mind.

A French teacher at school seemed to pick on me a lot in lessons, to the extent that the classmates in the French class felt sorry for me. I was very good at learning French with the previous French teacher in my early high school years, but when I moved into higher education, the new teacher spoiled it, and my moods festered deeper and I stopped learning French overnight and didn't even bother to take the exam in the end.

I also suffered a car crash which sent me into a traumatised state while staying with a friend at her aunty's house. My life flashed in front of me like an unravelled camera film of a whole lifetime of personal events. I survived the crash but let out banshee screams, and the friend's aunt refused to let me go home in fear she would be sued by my parents.

I guess it was a form of post-traumatic stress.

I was naïve and gullible as a teenager and easily led to stay quiet and get over things by myself. I do believe that the traumas which crossed my path made my mind muddles worse.

Physically, I had terrible issues of mixed needs. I was a virgin and I was brought up to be morally dignified within my Catholic faith and Mother's guidance, so the constant battle to control sexual urges was terribly difficult.

I constantly felt irritated in my nerves, and sexually pained. I lived my early teenage years in a fantasy bubble land and tried to stay away from mingling with youth, and only mixed with a couple of childhood friends. I briefly upheld a short-term social life. I went to a local community disco, and a nightclub, but only for experience not for desire.

Social Interaction

I was allowed go to discos and nightclubs at 15 years old. There were no formal identification requests in those young teenage years. Girls got away with entering adult social places by wearing heavy make-up and flashing a flirt and a smile. I became the wallflower in the room waiting for someone to chat to me. I experimented with lots of different alcoholic drinks and just like others I got drunk a lot but not drunk enough to lose my senses. I felt close to my senses deeply – sight, touch, smell, taste, hearing – which seemed more enhanced in high mood swing waves. I never liked the feeling of losing reality so tried to stay sensible while fitting in with the carefree teenage social lives of the disco 70s.

My father hurt my feelings badly, when I overheard him saying to his friend that he wished I was like my cousin in character. I think he was worried that I would bring shame to the family. He didn't realise that my cute sweet cousin was far more street wise as a townie. She educated me to not accept a joint when offered in a nightclub. She didn't really like fags, but she showed me how to light up my minty cigarettes, but I never dragged the smoke into my lungs. I am glad I didn't; it was easier to get bored from it and give up the social charade. Sadly there are ex school friends my age who have passed away from addictions too young. I much preferred playtimes with petal to the ugly vices of smoke and drink to ease off nasty moods.

I never went beyond a snog and a fumble when meeting young men in the nightclubs. There seemed to be respect from boys in those days, or maybe I was just lucky? I wasn't prepared to give my virginity to any one, he had to be a special one, and I knew God would guide me to the right man. My mother was an honourable woman and she instilled a sense of decorum in my teenage years, or maybe she just frightened me into thinking 'man' was a bad species to know, because my father never made her happy.

I felt for my mother; she put up with a lot of put downs gracefully. I have more fight in me and always need to have the last word, but I was grateful she taught me to wait, and I am proud to say that both my daughters are modest good girls and don't rush into a relationship.

I met my future husband, who crumbled my pure petal, from an army pen pal magazine. I had travelled to Germany to visit my brother who was stationed there and noticed an armed forces newspaper on his table. I jotted down the pen pal address and decided to apply for an army boyfriend – and I received over 40 replies from lonely young men.

One of the letters came from a very concerned brother who demanded to know what I was playing at. I think he felt I was thrown into the lion's den. Such brotherly love, I loved my bro's concern. I never listened to brother of course; I was a very stubborn sister.

I met my future husband – first on the list of would be suitors – and never looked beyond meeting him. I don't know what made me choose him. I was naturally attracted to dark-haired men, but he was a tall, fit, blonde, blue 'angel' eyed man. Maybe he sounded pure in his letters, maybe I sensed he would care for me, or maybe God – my best friend – told me he was meant to be; it was hard to tell from a photo. He certainly was chivalrous, getting down on one knee in front of my father and greeting me with a kiss on my hand. I wasn't looking my best, bedraggled and wet through, caught out from rain on the way back from work, make-up all stained and patchy, and clothes smelling of damp.

I walked in the house and Mother told me that my admirer had arrived, and I should go and tidy myself up. I answered her curtly that if he didn't like my appearance, he would be too shallow by nature, so he had to accept what he saw – a wet, stroppy, teenage girl.

We chatted over a hot dinner and I noticed his smile. I like a smile on a man for attractiveness. I feel that a man's soul shines from within his smile. I couldn't make up my mind whether I was really that attractive to him, I didn't feel any sexual tingling, no sparks of lust between us, no deep warm desire. I stared into his angel eyes and felt a deep dense thud in the pit of my stomach. The feeling was curdling and it wasn't pleasant. I am the sort of woman who turns a negative into a positive and thrives off challenge, so I couldn't understand why this gorgeous young man who was handsome, like a male version of an English rose, would make my stomach turn?

I felt my father breathing shallowly behind my back and sensed his concerns. Father gave me some advice a few days later, saying that foreigners were suited to other foreigners, and English people were cold in blood. I didn't listen to Father as foreigners didn't settle in our village and the Polish community were all elderly so there weren't any young men I could meet to please my father.

I was tired of the fights and character clashes that were constantly draining and causing Father to have terrible chest pains and high blood pressure. I really wanted to escape home and to be looked after, so I succumbed to Thomas for the wrong reasons. I decided he was the chosen one, and I was happy that Thomas had saved his virginity for me too. This wasn't helpful for sexual experience so in the long term we weren't suited to one another, and I didn't know at the time how difficult our future would be. I suffered more head turmoil because Thomas returned to Germany after his vacation and I spent eight months pining for him until he received a posting back home to England so we could marry.

I felt in my heart Thomas would be honourable and loyal. His naivety appealed to my own innocence. His parents were comfortable middle class. We fell into a relationship and marriage so quickly. We married in April 1979 and I became an army wife, living away from home at 17 years of age.

I hated the 19 years of marriage. I felt I had been robbed of my youth prematurely; I felt totally trapped and unloved. Not respected. Taken for granted. I was Rapunzel in an ivory tower, and I wanted to be Cinderella with a Prince Charming. Thomas didn't know how to please a woman. I knew on the morning after my wedding, my honeymoon wouldn't be memorable.

My new husband didn't want to make love during the honeymoon week. He said I had fat legs and dark hair, and he wanted me to have slim legs and a thinner figure and blonde hair. So why had he married me?

I was nothing like the description he desired. From then on I knew I wouldn't receive the passion my body yearned and desired to stabilise my moods.

Marriage and Children
Married at 17, pregnant at 19.

I wanted to adopt children; there were a lot of lonely parentless children in the world. My husband wanted to be a young dad, father his own flesh and blood. I wasn't ready for it, but when you love someone you want to give them everything.

The pregnancy went smoothly, and I gave birth in a cottage hospital in the Cotswolds. I delivered our baby with an orgasmic blast of a push, three hours in labour and out he came, my first born a son. I looked at this pure tiny baby perfectly formed with lovely skin and felt nothing maternally. I felt as if I had just expelled a solid wriggling lump and wondered how functional this solid lump would be as part of my life. I didn't feel rejection; I just didn't have a connection to the baby who was part of me and my husband. I felt freaky as if I was a baby carrier, and someone would collect the baby and take him away and my mind was terribly muddled, so many thoughts and sentences jumbling me.

I wanted to be pampered, to have food bestowed on me, and my family to look after me. My mind felt childlike, as if I was an infant again.

I feared the baby. I was embarrassed to be a new mum. I became unresponsive to the nurse's requests to breast feed my son. I didn't dislike my son, I thought he was gorgeous to look at, but I didn't feel as if he belonged to me, and I hadn't any emotional attachment to him.

Three days after giving birth I started to feel very confused. I felt agitated; I became repetitive in everything I did. I started to move about quickly, my brain was miles ahead of my body, or it was miles behind my body. I didn't feel I had a brain or a body sometimes. I just felt I was a gust of wind rushing from one job to another but getting nothing done. My senses were all jumbled. Life was rushing faster than I was living it. People on the television seemed to be reaching out to me, I felt they were talking to me, I thought I was being spied on. I kept hearing voices outside my ears. I heard planes drumming above my house, but we had left the armed forces and I was living back in my home village, so the flight path wasn't busy.

I was sure life outside my home was hostile. I didn't fit in with living amongst people. I convinced myself I was a freak, maybe an alien? and my self-worth was shredded. I was a failure as a mother.

I thought I could smell things that weren't in the room. I thought I could hear conversations outside my ears. I had difficulty to control over-eating, and sometimes I didn't eat at all, and I couldn't swallow food properly as if my co-ordination was haywire. Living day to day was disorientated, and most days I didn't have any motivation to eat, dress or wash and looked very unkempt and unattractive, and I smelt pungent.

My son needed attention and I just wanted to ignore him. I couldn't walk without falling over and I feared my home, I feared the environment in each room. Days progressed, and my emotions were rapidly changing, I felt anxious, happy, sad, moody, bubbly and tearful all at once. I was a robot with a memory going out of control into melt down. I was fortunate that my husband, and his mother, and my mother, were there to help with the baby in the first six months of his life. Time progressed, but I wasn't getting any better. I had a lot of support, but my mind wasn't calming down.

My sleeping pattern was continually broken and poor. I was in a bubble, like the bubbles you blow out of a looped stick, trapped, then floating in the air. The doctor said I had the baby blues – postnatal depression – but as I progressively got worse with bizarre behaviour like making a dozen cups of tea but not drinking them, and talking to the television and walls, the doctor decided I was suffering *Puerperal Psychosis* and referred me to a psychiatrist as my symptoms were worsening daily. Insanity was beckoning the Grim Reaper to move forward. My confusion turned to fear, and the devil had a grip on me. I felt it would be easier to die than to live this life of oblivious insanity. My love for my child stopped me from self-harm. My soul was decaying and I became lethargic and unco-operative; I felt unwanted, a leper, dysfunctional and weird.

My relationship with my husband deteriorated fast. We were flung into parenthood and stopped having special times together. He seemed only interested in playing with his son, and selfishly joined hobbies while I struggled to juggle being a mother and holding down a working life.

This scenario sounds like one faced by thousands of new young mums, but not all mums suffered the paranoia I suffered, and the oblivious state of mind I lived in. How I managed to cook food without causing a fire I will never know.

These feelings of despair and anxiety and surrealistic

existence lasted for a year and neither the general practice nor the psychiatric profession wanted to handle my poor mental health. When I became desperately ill mentally, I phoned both emergency services for support because my head spun into a fantasised state and the health authorities didn't seem to take me seriously. I tossed about between two health places like a ping pong ball on a table tennis table. The support network for mental health was incredibly poor in the early 1980s.

I felt lost, scared and disorientated. My mind suffocated. I thought people were shouting in my ears, and I believed that strangers would start stalking me and attack me.

There were times I didn't even realise I wasn't wearing any clothes, until I felt too cold and then suddenly realised I was naked. I randomly used to pick up my son from his cot and wake him up to play with his toys at 3am – to help me realise he was real, and I was real too.

My husband seemed ignorant, blasé, with little understanding of the womanly or motherly issues I faced. I felt he'd forgotten how young I was when he pulled me into his entangled web of little affection. He didn't know how to be tactile spontaneously. He didn't know how to handle a 'hot blooded' young woman, who was constantly trip wiring on her sex drive waves. He often mentioned he felt inadequate, that I was ignorant to his problems, that I didn't know how to compromise in our relationship or to heal it better. I thought that maybe giving our son a sibling would make husband happier; he was a hands-on father and he loved being a dad.

I ignored all doctors' advice about spacing out time to produce another child, and I became pregnant again within two years. I felt more experienced as a mother, so I was sure that my mental history wouldn't repeat itself.

Second Birth

My second pregnancy ran smoothly, and I felt more confident being pregnant; I seemed to bloom nicely. Husband and I were more experienced as parents. Our toddler was a beautiful happy child, a joy to us, and grandparents. My in-laws were tremendously supportive, I couldn't have wished for better grandparents. But my mother-in-law was very difficult to understand emotionally. She seemed a bitter woman, with a barrier around her, and the family group didn't seem to be as strong in caring for each other as mine were. My father-in-law was lovely; I liked him a lot. He was an honest down-to-earth man and you could see the love that shone through him that he had a grandson. I was quite stable in this period of carrying a second child. Scan machines evolved, and I found out I was carrying a second son. Husband left the army to give our children a more stable, rooted life. I liked the army wife life, but I respected my husband's wishes and settled into the village I was born and grew up in.

I was happy that my children would go through the same education route as I did. My parents were only a couple of streets away, and I felt emotionally secure with the support available. I didn't expect the events that unfolded in the eighth month of my pregnancy.

The month of May, a nice warm evening. I sat in my parents' garden talking to my mother. My son toddled clumsily along the path in the garden to his *dziadek*, his grandad, and fell over. I didn't rush to pick him up, my father was closer to him. Father scooped my son in his arms and scurried towards me, I saw his ruddy complexion becoming brighter, the sweat running down his cheeks as his face turned angry. I knew I was heading for yet another confrontational storm brewing.

Father wanted an excuse to shout again and I drew the unlucky straw. He was unhappy that I wasn't watching out for my son and had been too preoccupied with chatting to my mother. Father wanted to offload his own anxieties and failings on me and paint me as a bad mother. Father came up to me and put my son in my arms. I handed my son to my mother who went indoors with him and I braced myself for yet another explosive argument.

Father shouted and cursed me for not picking up my child off the floor; he inflamed so easily out of something so trivial. I retaliated by screaming back at him that he made my life a nightmare, and he never seemed caring towards me and my brothers when we were growing up. How could he tarnish me when I learnt the anger, the impulsiveness and the erratic behaviour from him? I decided to go indoors to bid Mother goodbye and take my son home but before I went, I approached Father and asked him for a plant pot which I needed to re-root a seedling in my home. He gave me one. My heart wanted to stretch my arms out and cuddle him, but I felt I couldn't – the moment was too tense and the pressures in the air were too stifling. I stared into his eyes and I felt humble and sad through eye contact with him. He bowed his head realising he had upset me, and I walked away. This was the last time I saw him alive.

Father died the next morning from a heart attack. I felt uncomfortable during the night, my chest was tight, I couldn't breathe, I was panicking. I woke my husband at 5am. I asked him to go and check on my father.

My husband wasn't happy, he wanted a bank holiday lie-in. I started to cry, so reluctantly he got up, and said he'd go for a run around the block and call in at 6am. However, before he had the chance to go, a young neighbour from my father's street knocked on the door. He'd come on his motorbike to inform us my mum was hysterical. My husband told me there was an emergency in our home, and all I could do was wait till he got back. Half an hour later my husband returned and said my father had died. When he'd got to the house my mother was cradling my father in her arms. Father still felt warm, so my husband tried to perform resuscitation, but failed to revive him. He came home distraught to break the news that my father was dead. I screamed, I shouted, I clenched my fists. I broke down, I slumped into a confused haze. The strength of emotional family bonding is so harrowing, there seems no end to the grief for a parent's death. I was heading for a complete breakdown, a trip through a dark tunnel of insanity.

My second son was born on the day of my father's funeral, amongst a hail of rain, thunder and lightning at 4.30am with rain and wind beating on my bedroom window.

The most harrowing traumatising emotion I could feel when I lay exhausted from giving birth, was a very deep grey blankness of not knowing what was happening to me. I didn't know if I would come out of the delirious state. My eyes glazed, my body rigid. I was entombed within a comatose oblivion; I had no idea where I was heading. I was lost in space, in a black hole, and the world around me was a dizzy haze.

Hormones

Hormones change within us all the time, through emotional dramas, traumas, ageing, ill health, and influences of people and the environment. The head is the headquarters of all our emotions – the signal box that sends out the transmitting messages of how we behave and interact and feel. The mind is the communicator which makes decisions for us, so if one is born with a complexed confusing mind, it makes the body walk blindly and act strangely. I know that my mind triggered bipolar through the action of childbirth, because my body is made up of a lot of progesterone, which dropped quickly when I gave birth too quickly.

I gave birth within four hours and too much oestrogen had to compensate for the loss.

My sex nerves were on fire and jumbled my brain like an erogenous volcanic outburst.

Puerperal psychosis changed into manic depressive craziness which is now known as bipolar. Bipolar comes in several forms and I inherited bipolar 1 with psychotic tendencies, which I manage to keep under control, as best as I can with blips triggering unpredictably.

No one knew at the time I had more than one illness, and that was the reason why many tablets didn't seem to control me unless I was heavily sedated and sleepy, causing lethargic dysfunction. I needed to be functional because I was a mother, so the psychiatry profession needed to find the right balance of tablets, not knowing that I had other mental health and personality issues.

I struggled with the crazy swings for many years when nothing seemed to work to help me be functional in society.

Traumatic Labour

The birth of my second son was unexpected. I needed the bathroom in the early hours, I was deeply lost in my head and I didn't realise my son's head had started to materialise through my petal. I thought I was passing faeces, but a shout from my husband startled me. He had followed me to the bathroom to check I was ok. He saw the crown of the head appearing as I strained to pass and forcibly picked me up by my arms and threw me on the bed. My son shot out of my body and my husband caught him. The lightning flashed through the rain teared bedroom window as the premature helpless bundle spluttered to gasp his first breath. Husband cleared his airwaves and left him on my stomach with umbilical cord still attached. We didn't own a phone to call a doctor at 4am, so husband left me lying with our baby, attached to the umbilical, on my bare stomach. He went to my mother's house to tell her and my brother (who had come to stay for the funeral) that I needed a doctor. My mother lived two streets away from us.

My local doctor and my mother arrived at my home at the same time. They entered the bedroom and I stared at them in a fixed glaze. No words came out of my mouth, I didn't know if I was grieving for a death or celebrating a life; the two dramas collided and disturbed my head thoughts. The doctor cut the umbilical cord and asked if I wanted to keep it; I didn't respond. It was a strange feeling. I heard his words, I understood his words, but I couldn't speak and answer him. The doctor wrapped the cord in a sheet and the ambulance arrived to take my baby son to a premature baby unit. He was five weeks premature. The ambulance crew wrapped him in foil and sheet.

The sight of a young ambulance man looking at my near naked body made me feel uncomfortable and I jerked out a few words of disapproval. I whispered he was too young to be in the room to witness a birth and he informed me he was over 18 and had seen plenty of mothers with rushed births. I whispered a tired "thank you" and knew my son would be cared for in hospital. I hadn't named him, and at that moment in time I really thought I was heading the same way as my father. I couldn't feel the use of my legs and I felt as if I was in a state of suspended animation. I didn't feel as if I was real.

My tiny son was taken to hospital because his lungs were underdeveloped. My husband told me that he had named him on my behalf. The only Polish name on the list of half a dozen boys names we had chosen together. For once my husband was sensitive and respectful of the Polish culture I was born into. I was happy my second son was given a Polish name. I smiled weakly. The doctor turned to my mother and, putting his arms around her to comfort her, said:

"A soul departs from our world and another soul enters to replace it."

His words etched my lost mind. I have never forgotten those comforting words. I will never forget my spiritual soulful GP, and I truly believe that souls evolve – but not in the same patterns of life.

The next day a psychiatrist came to assess me; it was my first meeting with an exceptionally tall man. His name was Dr K, my new psychiatrist. I really hoped he would find a way to keep the brainwaves under control. He advised my husband to take me into hospital for assessment.

This was my first experience of entering a mental institution. I was too zombified to feel fear or refuse.

Manic Madness Monster House

We approached the overwhelming grounds of an intimidating huge Victorian hospital building. I didn't know where I was going; I was slumped in the car motionless. I couldn't differentiate speed, so the traffic was either in slow motion or speeding by or both. I felt I was controlling the traffic lights, and my eyes were changing the sequence. I felt powerless and weightless. I seemed to have lost my mind and couldn't feel my body; my personality disappeared and spirit perished. My head was fazed, spinning in all directions, and I felt like a ghost holding my head under my armpit. The mind, body and head thoughts were all in disarray. I could only obey the command of my husband like an android dolly. The building looked lethargic, creepy, dismal and sad. The atmosphere screamed a million deaths.

The feeling of isolation and terror within me heightened, my heart pumping, my legs buckling as I walked the long hallway, my husband leading me, arms linked in an uncomfortable grip. The atmosphere felt secretive, strange and sinister.

Paint peeling off walls and urinal smells constantly drifted and the air breathed a wilderness of danger and torment. I sensed cold air vibes and little electric shocks which made my arm hairs stand and feel sore.

We climbed endless stairs and eventually came to a room I was going to call home for three months.

I looked at the floor through my hazy state of oblivion, and images of lions stared back at me through the mingled orange, brown and red hues. This was the first experience of *pareidolia*, a mind disorder I never knew I had. I could see shaped images when my mind felt enhanced. I didn't feel scared of the lions, I felt comforted, and with owning the zodiac sign of Leo upon birth, I thought the carpet lions might protect me from unsavoury patients.

I spent a lot of time looking at the floor in the asylum. Men patients sitting in the communal living room made me very tense. I sensed that these people would be challenging, and I felt vulnerable because of my age – I was only 22 years old at the time. I didn't realise that dangerous people were housed in a more secure unit nearby. Fear grasped my throat, worry and insecurity swamped me. Maybe patients might attack me?

My children might not be allowed to visit me?

I felt very lonely and my husband seemed distant with me. He exchanged my personal information with the ward Matron and told me he was going.

I never received a kiss, nor encouragement that things would be ok. My husband cast me aside like a worn-out rag left to be mopped up by the carers.

I was human! a mother! a wife! a loving woman! and my head wanted to scream these thoughts out loud, but my mouth remained shut, as husband left without a word. He was relieved to leave me there.

Feelings

I know I have a strong extraordinary perception of feelings from the environment. I see vibes in the air, space shifting constantly as we evolve in our daily living. I feel pressures particularly at night time, as if the dark unknown is trying to squeeze the life out of me, which brings on discomfort physically from my gut and lower abdomen. Once I am up and about functioning in my daily routine I feel much better, as if the light of the day has washed away the pain of the night.

I won't let the sensations drain my life away. I am here for a purpose on this Earth and I will keep moving and stay strong for as long as my soul feels it needs to be grounded in this confusing shell of a body I own. I also feel that my sense of hearing has been deadened over the years, I feel I haven't been allowed to hear everything I should. My vision is poor due to heredity short-sightedness, but I am sure a couple of my senses must be substandard to let the other senses be more acute and perceptive.

My husband left the hospital ward and he offloaded the responsibility of my illness into the care of the hospital. The worst feeling when being in a building that smelt of doom was not knowing if I would be let out again or held imprisoned for life. Classed as insane. Never to see my family again. These sorts of feelings made my body feel hollow, my mind just thin air, and my life non-existent. Mummified. Forgotten. Neglected.

The Patients

The first patient I noticed in the hospital was a young bespectacled man in his mid-twenties. He looked like a character I remembered in the 1960s children's television programmes. The intelligent little blonde guy in a huge chair with large spectacles. He sat in a world of his own staring up to the ceiling, hands clasped together, rocking forwards and backwards. He didn't speak to anyone, he seemed to be cocooned in his own world, trying to cope with his head thoughts silently.

A middle-aged woman skipped over to me, she looked dotty, she acted potty. She reminded me of the flower power hippies and kept chanting she wanted to hug a tree, and kiss the moon, and do a happy dance.

"He won't talk," she said. *"He has been here three weeks, and no one can make him talk, not even his parents."* She looked at me, child-like, as if she expected me to perform a miracle of communication. No chance of that happening, I could barely talk myself; the locked jaw syndrome must be infectious when insane and lost in a bricked head maze.

I felt a prod in my side. An unkempt tousled-haired young woman started to stroke and touch my arm and feel my head.

"Do you want to undress me?" she sounded pitiful.

She started to undress in front of me, and I began to copy her and started to undress myself. I seemed to have got drawn into her stance and movement and the magnetic waves between us encouraged me to be her mirror opposite.

A male nurse stepped between us.

"Not here ladies." He sounded authoritative with a friendly smile. I sensed he was ok. I knew when I felt threatened by someone and when I felt comfortable; at least that wasn't stripped from me when my mind blipped into oblivion.

A male senior patient drooling from his lips, lurched forward full on face contact, his tablet doped eyes locked into my green hazed ones.

"You're pretty," he leered, *"kiss please?"* spitting at me in the process of his request for affection.

The nurse linked my arm and led me to my dormitory, and gratefully I walked away from the strange patients. I was shown my bed and my blood pressure checked, the contents of my bag counted, and then I was left alone.

A little later a female nurse brought me some tablets and a jug of water. The nurse didn't give me an explanation of what sort of tablets I was taking. She handed me a plastic tumbler, poured the water, stood over me and scrutinised the way I held the tablets. She watched me swallow the tablets, she checked my mouth and tongue, and then she bustled away. I slithered into the bed and fell into a deep sleep. I awoke later, and my stomach immediately sank. I knew I was hidden away and still alone, no one in the other beds…

Worry came over me.

I really hoped I was waking up in my own home, my toddler son jumping on my bed. Husband at work. No, it was still dark, still the same evening, still the same cesspit, still the same fears – and the loneliness made me want to nail myself into a coffin and wait for direction into the afterlife.

I was incarnated into a ghostly form. Time was infinite, no beginning no end, and not a clock in sight.

Life in a mental institution is harsh without time.

The daily routine was simple. Awake in the morning, vacate bed, wash and dress, breakfast, medication, dinner, tea, medication, supper, medication again, bed.

Endless hours by myself, and health check assessments. Student doctors visited for long drawn out conversations. Blood pressure and blood tests were taken regularly. If the unlucky short straw was drawn, there was a trip to 'memory-loss lane', otherwise known as ECT (electroconvulsive therapy).

I was saved from 'memory-loss lane'. When my husband finally turned up to visit me, I told him that I was going to have my brains blown out in electrocution, he'd never recognise me as his wife again, and I wouldn't remember my kids again. I said I would be wheeled down death row if he signed the dotted line on my behalf.

I must have scared him enough for him to voice his concerns to senior staff, and I was saved from mind frazzling. Never having to experience that custom. EVER. Thankfully.

Husband must have loved me a little to have saved my personality. I am grateful for that. Thank you ex hubby.

Lost

During the hospital stay, my mind surreally floated, my vision and perspective of life became severely distorted. I found it hard to trust the staff in the hospital. The nurses' attitudes were different daily. Nurses were understanding, then not understanding. Caring, not caring. Efficient and not efficient. Kind and unkind. Daunting, superior, strict, power mad and sometimes perverse.

The nursing staff seemed to have different moods when it suited them. I never knew how they would behave towards me every time they were on shift.

The hospital ward was a horrible situation to be in; I was trapped in an ugly hellish building, and constantly felt the death of people within the walls because my deep feeling of empathy was enhanced greatly in psychosis. I was shivering in the freezing cold atmosphere.

I felt I needed to watch over my shoulder constantly, which raised anxiety levels and fearfulness daily. I trembled with anticipation at the start of each nursing shift. I felt vulnerable and nerve-wracked with a paralysed conscience of despair, not knowing how my day would evolve. The nursing staff communicated with disturbed patients using similar eye contact techniques, which I found irritating, intrusive and intimidating, staring at patients forcefully.

They knew how to eyeball a patient into submissive passivity when needed. I felt all the nurses' body heat – they all seemed to live off a high sex drive – and I absorbed their heat when they bustled around me. They seemed to feel excited when dealing with patients but, at the same time, presented an authoritative exterior of professionalism and control. I often wondered if they were taking toilet breaks for a fag or a jerk off.

I experienced a lot of massages but I never asked for them. I would be told to go to my room and a male nurse would massage my shoulders from behind me. I found it pleasant but strange, and then he'd go. During regular daily health checks, a nurse performed blood tests, or blood pressure readings, and seemed to press a breast into my face to the point of me feeling suffocated, and then she'd release the breast and stare at my eyes and let me go. When I developed bad panic moments and my mind couldn't cope with reality, the nurses asked me to lie on the bed and my breasts were massaged by a male nurse and a female nurse, then they would go off together. Where? Who knows? I just know it left me lying there more confused than when I was admitted. Maybe these acts were acts of kindness – a form of stimulation to keep you *real* in mind? Maybe the nurses were slightly cuckoo themselves to hold down a vocation in a mad hospital and were expressing excessive emotional steam. I will never know. The whole of the mentally ill hospital ward exuded a feeling of 'neediness' from both nursing staff and patients. The only person who wasn't needy was myself, but I was hopelessly lost. That's all. Three months stay for my first trip. I hoped I wouldn't experience it again. I did. Time and time again for over a decade, a vicious merry-go-round carousel of crazy mind devilish self-affliction, of lost control – because my mind was too youthful to understand how to STAY IN CONTROL.

'Oddities' so make the change!

There is a link in my mood cycles to seasonal light changes. I go bipolar high in spring between the middle of March and the middle of June, and again middle of September to middle of November. I can only assume the light lowering or rising through GMT time changes sends error messages to my brain, and without thinking about it I start feeling loopy thoughts, seeing loopy things, sensing loopy changes, hearing loopy things and smelling loopy things. Conclusion, life has circled some loopy loops in my life span when manic tendencies have blipped. I am still here though. That's good news.

Hope for me, hope for all.

Examples of some symptoms I have experienced include ranting incoherently and feeling grandeur. Chanting. Listening to music obsessively with decibels exceeding ear health safety. Wanting to spend money all day. (If there's no credit card and not much in the bank, you cannot. Best place to be is poor.) Feeling scared of the immediate environment, scared of people, feelings of being watched, seeing unusual figure-shaped shadows – visualising things that aren't there.

When stretched ears were all the rage, as a fashion accessory, I maniacally flipped on one occasion when I saw a staff member in a well-known fast-food chain restaurant with a stretched ear. I stared at him and thought the Martians had landed, and then I thought everyone in the establishment wasn't real and all were aliens adopting human bodies. It is easy to get lost in hyper moments. Body mannerisms act fast, voice speed increases, energy levels blast into space, no sleep at night, I lose co-ordination skills. SUGGESTION: good time to avoid cooking, housework, people, LIFE.

Lie down and think happy thoughts, stare at the clouds, watch the sunset, have a relaxing bath. You must learn to love yourself, to deal with yourself, to deal with life. Make the change.

Change your routine, do something worthwhile for others, feel functional, pray, go to church, join a club, talk to the

Samaritans, a counsellor, community nurse, doctor, your parent, your sibling, your close friend. Be creative, write a story, your story, do a poem, draw a picture, paint, go for long walks, join the gym, do something good for charitable causes. Never say I cannot do it. You can! You will. You must try, for the sake of your own self-respect, self-esteem, and family who need you. Families suffer too. Soul destroying insanity destroys relationships. Think positive.

Redeem control and reality.

Record your feelings, write them down, list your favourite songs, listen to the ones you know that will make you strong within yourself. The song that helped me the most in my pitiful times, was the ballad *The Greatest Love of All*, which made me feel love.

The warm inner feeling of strength feels wonderful; it compresses each side of your stomach into pleasurable sensations in your belly button. If it's never happened you haven't found the song that makes you feel whole. The soul in the stomach behind the belly button. Soul feels good, you feel good. Your belly feels wonderful. And here's everyone thinking the changes must only be in the mind. No. The mind starts the changes, to make the change in the belly.

The belly. The real definition of a belly laugh is when laughter, giggles and happiness within a belly make a person a happier being. When you are happy, your belly feels lighter, no matter how heavy you are. When you are depressed, your belly feels heavy – it feels like a deadened pit. I noticed when I carry heavy shopping that, if I feel low, the heaviness is hard for my fingers and hands; but when I feel happy, the same amount of shopping feels easier to manage and the load is not a burden. Sayings like 'take the weight off your shoulders' are there for a reason and so is the phrase 'have a belly laugh'. The soul shines within your belly. If the belly doesn't make you feel happy, try relaxation from the mind – meditation is a wonderful thing.

Be aware of your daily activities. The things you eat. The things you talk about in conversation, the things you do. If you feel any discontent at any time of the day or night, think what it might relate to, make a note. Maybe the same reason for the same negative feelings will crop up again another day. If so, you will know what to squash, to change, to make a difference.

Self-awareness of the symptoms of bipolar and other mental illnesses is the key to being in control. You cannot cure it, but you can keep it at bay. You can. You will. I know you will.

Stay in control. Please.

Pareidolia and other Phenomena

I have an unusual mind for seeing pictures in things all around me. This is called pareidolia. My mind sees patterns in random memory. I have seen faces and animals in the clouds. I have seen distorted faces of people as if they were squashed in solid items like a pavement or trees and leaves. I saw Pope John Paul the Polish Pope in the clouds, and I see things in all sorts of places like in the air of a dark night and in steamed windows. I saw a dark angel of death in the sky and I see genes floating in the air, and orbs too.

One day I woke up early morning and a light shone down from my ceiling in a tubular beam; inside the light were hundreds of moving shapes, which looked like tiny genes that you see under a microscope. There was another light, a square white light shape near my door which I believe could have been the energy of a deceased relative.

I am convinced that God can transform into lights, shapes and orbs. I believe God came to me as an orange orb when I was praying by my bed one night. An orange orb entered my room glowing, hovered over me while I was praying and disappeared. I can see animals in soap bubbles too and pictures of unusual things in people's photography.

I believe my mind is complex and special and my attitude to people who call me a nutter is that they aren't special enough. The non-believers of everything will become nothing when they die. I believe I will rise again somehow, somewhere, as something special again. My hearing is just as acute and sensitive, and I can hear talking from nowhere, I can hear myself answering myself back and I hear cat noises frequently when my own cat is sleeping peacefully. Cats are special. Many countries believe that cats are reborn from great human beings, especially in middle eastern royalty.

I can also see ghosts, but I choose not to most of the time. I find them visually upsetting so choose to switch off my sense of sight in ghostly surroundings and feel the ghost in awareness instead. I've seen a Victorian lady walking past me with a black dog; I know she was a ghost because she floated, and the dog was an apparition. I have also heard ghostly sounds and doors opening and shutting in a local pub. In another pub, I felt someone was constantly standing behind me who didn't exist. I once met a funeral director and he told me he often sees ghosts when dealing with the dead in the funeral parlour. He told me this over a cup of tea and I told him of my experiences and then both of us looked at the light bulb and the light dimmed and re-shone again in front of us.

I used to hear a child running up and down the balcony of a house I used to live in. I got used to hearing it but there was no one because I always kept the door open, so the person would have had to cross my doorway. After investigation locally, I found out a little boy had been killed running down the back of the alley, chasing after his ball. The alley was at the end of my backyard and he ran head-long into a delivery truck at the bottom of the alley. I presumed the boy had lived in a house where my house was built, in the early 1940s war years he was born in.

I have also experienced things in a high state of mania. I smashed a wine glass to smithereens that stood behind me on a kitchen surface, with no heat near it. I have made a brass handle of a door slam down with my eyes which scared me enough to take the doors off in the living room. I was worried at that time I would become a living poltergeist.

I have also seen shadow ghosts, shadow cats and shadow dogs. I feel that psychic people have super senses and enhanced emotions and there's a choice to ignore or stifle a psychic gift or learn how to use it wisely. Stifling a gift results in mental unbalance. Using a gift unwisely causes distress to others but using it wisely can be beneficial to lots of people. The key is to learn all you can about your capabilities and turn them positively to your health benefit.

Many people can do what I can do, so googling things can teach you a lot because you can be sure that someone somewhere will have written about their personal experiences. Never be afraid of being different to other people. What is normal? We are all born with individual unique blueprint genetically and we must respect other people's characters and habits, and if we cannot stomach someone, walk away. That's the best way.

Angels, Time dimensions, God and Shapeshifters

I believe in angels; I believe there are celestial people among us who spiritually breathe well-being through air and attach themselves to humans who are receptive and there are earth angels who are fallen angels of light and dark who walk amongst us in human form and act accordingly to the light or dark side of their characters. I can feel angels in public, either by eye contact with them or by the wind energy that breezes from their body. An earth angel always acknowledges me if they walk past me as a stranger so, equally, they must tune into my special energies within.

The strangest thoughts within me are my origins before I became 'matter'. I believe I was the East Wind god, who was EURUS amongst the Greek mythology wind deities. That is such an ego-heavy proclamation to make when I stated I wasn't even a prophet. My extreme energy within is a wind, fighting crazy electrical brainwaves. I googled the four wind gods of the Earth and it says the East Wind god symbolises poetry and literature, things which I have always held in my heart and life span.

My empath abilities go beyond man and I stand firm in what I believe. My father named me *Boguslawa* (Goddess) at birth; a name I always felt uncomfortable with and renounced when I organised my adult passport. My soul is a formed energy of air power combined with a strong electrical current of my human make-up. I believe we are all made up from matter from planets and my matter is from Jupiter because the aurora borealis (Northern Lights) are special to me.

Having empath abilities mustn't be confused with having empathy for someone; the two words are similar but have different meanings.

I have deep perception of sixth sense emotions, but equally as a human I seem to project very little empathy or understanding of others and distance myself from people. I believe I protect my health and other people's health by living a disconnected life within humanity. There are many people who have proclaimed their talents and characters, but we are often classed as weird or ill when we are gifted creative intelligent people.

There are supernatural beings, 'shapeshifters', who can change shape. I witnessed a shapeshifter in an old cinema toilet in my town. I had gone to see the remake of *The Magnificent Seven* and a vision appeared in the mirror as I washed my hands. This felt very unsettling. I stared into the mirror and said, *"Sorry, am I in your way?"* and moved towards the door, when I turned back the vision had changed to a dwarf old woman who giggled *"It's alright"*. A lot of people would have run out screaming or would have been shocked. I just burst into tears in the hallway and a cinema attendant asked if I was ok.

People can remember historical events in hypnotic regression and sense the feel of a place, area or building as being somewhere before. We are time travellers, those who are blessed with the knowledge and capability of knowing their core within. I have witnessed time repeating itself too when my children were young on the way to school. I saw a car drive fast and turn into another road and people shouting out of the window. The next day I witnessed the same car, same situation, same words, and same cars following that car.

I believe in time overlapping and quantum leaps in past and future, and what is time anyway? Figures of a clock and calendars were invented by humans so there was structure in the way we organise our lives to be functionally synchronised, but do we live in reality? Are we victims of our own surreal world, and perceive only what we choose to perceive? All people have an energy field, everyone can achieve great things; that's why so many people have shown great strength and courage and carried out great feats. Believe in faith and strive with drive. Achieve. Bring out your inner intuitive talents for positive good causes.

Break Down Again

Mother's death happened unexpectedly. She died after a visit to my aunty who lived in the town. I completely tipped up, tipped over, crashed down. My head just went out of control, I was lost in thought again. Mother suffered a heart attack while rushing to the bus stop. The day was a bank holiday and buses were infrequent. She had a hearty meal with her cousin, my aunt, and the day turned out totally unexpected.

I was in a different county for a lovely day at a theme park with husband and our sons and came back to a policeman standing outside our house. I screamed, I bellowed, I clenched my fists. I slammed the table hard. My mind submitted to a state of self-oblivion. No one notices at first what is happening to a bipolar head, because the body performs routine family domestic chores as normal, so husband expected me to get over Mother's death because I still performed household duties.

My brothers arrived with their families as soon as they were free to do so, and we all met up at my mother's house before the funeral. I can remember walking into the house and then I started spinning around and around in my head and in my body, my head spinning one way, my body spinning the opposite way, like a waltzer ride at a fairground. I fell over in front of my grieving family.

My mother's death traumatised me so much I was starting to lose my mind again. Erratic mind waves are not easy to control if neuron cells are imbalanced.

I wept through Mother's funeral service, and I couldn't face seeing my mother lowered into her grave; I turned my back in grief, and family and friends felt sadness at my actions.

When the funeral ended, I got progressively worse. I worked on a delicatessen counter of a major high-street store, and I tried to keep busy and focused. I think, looking back on it, that I should have taken time off work, but I wanted to keep motivated – it's important to keep busy when unstable or the oblivious illness manifests itself badly. I found out that two members of staff had lost their mothers to unexpected death and the saying was that things happen in threes. My mother was the third death in that May week. I thought I could cope. I couldn't. Towards the end of the shift the counters had to be cleaned, and I started to become dreamy in my head.

I sang the Polish national anthem at the top of my voice, while cleaning the counter. I lost my job, because I didn't tell the manager I was prone to mental instability. At home, I kept taking my clothes off, trying to go naked down the street, I threw money into the garden to feed God. I saw visions on television, my deceased aunty shaking a baby, my brother shaking a toy rabbit, and royalty remarrying each other but with different partners.

I began to suffer pareidolia more often.

I visualised pictures in everything I looked at, and my eyes felt that things around me were distorted, I was in my own bubble of madness thought. I made endless cups of coffee and tea and left them undrunk. I thought I was queen of the world and my sons were kings of England and Poland, and I caused a huge debt on a credit card by buying things I didn't need. Husband called time on my actions and admitted me back into the same mental hospital and ward as previously. I followed him meekly and dazed, my head hung in shame.

I was a crazy soul and ostracised again.

I came out of my amnesic, zonked out state two days later, and a nurse showed me a woman in another part of a building. She was a mother of eight children, and she was just spinning around in circles in the corridor. The nurse told me if I bred more children, that would happen to me, as the woman had been there three years and had never come out of the trance.

This period in hospital was a bad time for me. I collapsed a few days later traumatised. I fell into a deep trance, and I think my blood pressures collided. The emergency medical team placed me on a bed, put a drip into my arm and started to rub and pummel my whole body: my arms, my legs, my chest. I remember levitating, a yellow glow in the top right-hand corner of the ceiling was pulling me closer, my body was on the ground, but my thoughts were in the air. I could see myself on the bed with medical staff around me. I was experiencing an outer body levitation. I remember thinking, *God take me if you want, but please to let my boys grow strong and healthy.*

The light brightened and then I felt air pressure pushing me back down to my body, and I stirred awake. God didn't want me this time. This was the second time I had cheated death, as I had been in a car crash when 15 years old and my life flashed back in picture form like a flip book that you roll between your fingers to see the character moving at different paces. These phenomena do happen; it all happened to me.

People I saw in previous hospital stays were readmitted at

the same time as me – we all seemed to be on the same seasonal madcap cycles. The young bespectacled man who never spoke became my pal. I managed to get him to talk because I wanted to befriend him, and my smile seemed to arouse his interest to converse. I persuaded him to hatch an escape plan from hospital with me for a laugh, and he came out of his shell to plan the great escape with me. We cheekily did a daredevil walk out of the ward after lunch and nobody stopped us. We walked to the city centre and then got lost, in a concrete flat estate. We finally found our way back to the hospital when teatime was over and we got scolded like two young school kids. Thereafter, my intelligent friend was always chatting to me – his parents were happy and my doctor gave me praise for giving him confidence.

I became firm friends with tree-hugging dotty lady too; she was bubbly like me and visited me in my home between hospital stays. A lady with haunting eyes taught me to play table tennis and we bonded through that, but I couldn't make her happy; she remained sad and she constantly looked soul lost, as if she had died a death, decaying. She couldn't discuss her anxieties, she kept them locked in and I felt her sinking spirit descending in every step she took, and every word she spoke. Table tennis was good though, something to do and she was champion at it. We promised each other we would meet up when we were well enough to join civilisation outside the hospital safe zone. I wanted to be her friend. She needed one.

The trips to the hospital were repeated for over a decade, twice a year every year as I fell victim to repeated insanity. I felt institutionalised and I started to lose friendships to death in the hospital – all sorts of untimely deaths – because those friends couldn't cope.

Patients would silently eat their meals, and after tea find ways to find permanent peace. The nursing staff couldn't be on independent watch for all patients so there were many opportunities to be left alone to plot a one-way road trip to eternity.

People also called time on their lives after leaving the hospital and my dear table tennis friend chose to end hers too; I was gutted. She didn't even wait to meet up with me. I read in the paper that on the day she cancelled our meeting she decided to cancel her life. I felt I hadn't done enough to save her. It was an enormous feeling of madness all around, to witness the deaths of people I had spoken to an hour before in hospital, and wave goodbye permanently to those dismissed. I expected my time to end in a disturbed twist too.

To be insane is great pain and scary.

The feeling of a tormented mind squeezes your stomach. The soul feels suffocated. Death is craved.

I was very fortunate to still have a spiritual connection to God, and I believe my faith and my strict Catholic upbringing saved me from losing my life, as in Catholicism it is a great sin to take your own life.

I also felt I had fantastic mental health support in the hospital, and I have a great admiration for two men who spent years counselling and helping me to believe in myself and cross the insanity hurdles with strength.

Dr H. was my Doctor of Hope; he was a lecturer at a university, but he spent his spare time chatting to mentally ill people, encouraging them to feel better within themselves, and making them feel special and worthy. Doctor of Hope was a dashing dark-haired man, articulate and dignified with a calming influence and a lovely smile.

Our first meeting was slightly annoying. I had heard that he was a pharmacist who experimented on animals to create pills for sick people. I had a strop on meeting him and threw my shoes at him in defence of the rodents he worked with. After that episode I accepted his friendship as it was boring in the hospital and he seemed to have a lot of thoughtful time for me. I am so glad we bonded as he developed an idea of cognitive therapy that included a written chart for me to be aware of the symptoms of the illness and to remember to take tablets for the symptoms. We spent hours discussing the chart. I was destitute, I really didn't know how to control my illness and the chart helped me with stability and self-awareness. I was in love with Doctor of Hope; he encouraged me to listen to him and I developed a passionate 'longing' reason to consciously act upon his advice to follow the chart. I don't know if he realised how I held a candle burning in his honour, but I will always feel a soft spot for him in thought, for the rest of my life.

Dr K. was my psychiatrist Doctor of Encouragement. He was a handsome fellow too, so tall and willowy. After my second son was born, he diagnosed me with manic depression (which eventually name changed to bipolar disorder). He told me from the beginning not to be afraid, that I was normal, and to always release anxiety, tension, head thoughts, and to never lock anything inside. He advised me to have faith and stay in control. Wonderful advice, a wonderful doctor, I was so lucky to have my super heroes looking after me. It is very important to have faith in the medical team caring for you. One must believe in their job to help the mentally ill to a road of recovery. I put all my trust in the two special doctors, and I will always feel in debt to their compassion and care because I know I was a very difficult, insane, fragile person in those days.

Family

My family found it very hard to understand me. Mental illness was the sort of thing that never seemed serious to them; they seemed to think that people brought it upon themselves, that they should snap out of it. Sometimes you know your family loves you, but they cannot handle you. They don't know how to make you better or what to say and do, to make things right. Life can be so lonely in the throws of unbalanced health when the stigma is so strong and brushed under the carpet.

To have faith is the greatest gift next to love. Sometimes love can feel as if it's gone, but if you believe in having faith, it can stay with you forever. To have faith is only dealing with your own strength, whereas love can be many things, and hurtful at times. I never felt that God was failing me, I believed that God wanted strong people and for people to be challenged. I was glad I was brought up within a spiritual environment – it made my soul stronger.

"Faith is the substance of things hoped for, the evidence of things not seen"

Hebrews 11:1

Time for a New Head

There comes a point where something happens, and you reach rock bottom. Mine happened on the eve of my birthday in 1989. I had an insanity moment and found myself in a locked room. There was only a bed and a mattress. Nothing else in the room. A tiny barred window and a heavy door with a hatch. I was stripped naked. I do not recall how the maniacal blip happened. My marriage was suffocating me. I felt let down by lack of affection and lovemaking, I felt my sex drive was overpowering me into madness. I had reached the stage of chewing the end of my pillows and waking up to feathers in my mouth. The gnawing sensations of frustrated desires unfulfilled were creating delusions: severe psychotic mania.

I was on a high level of different tablets. I was addicted to Temazepam which was prescribed for insomnia. My head reached a level of such high energy and my body was struggling to keep up with it. I blanked my thoughts. I had no existence, I felt I was three dimensional. I had a body I couldn't feel, I had stepped out of it, and I felt my energy had turned into an outline of my figure next to me. Empty shell body. I was thin air and an energy line of a figure by my side. The energy plasma was blending itself around my body giving me orgasmic sensations that were electrocuting my petal. My petal was a frazzle of delight, but my mind was deadened, I was a lost cause. I had cut myself into three areas of being. Whatever happened to me, my consciousness lost reality completely, and I just awoke in the hospital again, not knowing how I got there, in the safe cell.

A padded cell.

"Happy Birthday Kate," matron said with a bowl of breakfast porridge in her hand. *"Here's your breakfast, and your clothes, our Kate's back!"*

I started to like matron, she was like a surrogate mother figure to me. Authoritative but cheerful. I can remember thinking: *"I am not going to come back next time. It's my birthday, and I am naked in an empty room with porridge."* I should have been home celebrating my birthday with my sons. My husband visited me a couple of days later and told me I had overdosed on tablets. I had rung the Samaritans in a turmoiled desperation. The police had come to my aid and found me slumped in bed. I was sent straight to the psychiatric hospital who brought me round and placed me in the padded cell.

I spent my time in hospital writing stories. I started to write an educational story based around a tree house, but my original draft writings disappeared before I left the hospital, and then two decades later my tales were used in computer education. I can only presume an American psychiatric nursing auxiliary had taken my ideas and used them to create books. I continued to keep stimulated by writing at home; it made me feel good, but it was difficult to be accepted in publishing in those days, so my stories were never published, and became lost as I changed computers.

Writing helped me to stay focused and relieved my head of tormented thoughts and I was able to resist the mental anguishes I felt within. I felt power with a pen in my hand, and strong with the paper I was writing on. Putting colour on paper by drawing pretty things made me happy too. I realised my happiness was with art and craft – and writing.

Voluntary Work

I regained my confidence to be amongst people by helping in a charity shop. I had lost confidence because of the stigma attached to being mentally ill. Ignorant people in my village would ostracise me by walking on the other side of the road. My relatives switched off from my problems. They saw it as my husband's responsibility and my problem. They didn't understand how to help tackle the madness and hoped it would go away. No one can walk in your shoes, only you, yourself.

I became strong, I confronted my own mind. I didn't want to go to hospital or to eat porridge, naked, alone on my birthday, ever again. I was determined to find something to occupy the mind. I joined the local scout group. The best thing I did to make the life change fruitful. I put all my energy and creativeness into establishing educational activities for young children to enjoy. I was driven and I created more than one group, and lived and breathed the educational programmes I created. My husband was already a scout leader so we both had something in common. The self-esteem I gained progressed to gaining employment too. While I was a scout leader, I managed to stabilise my moods. I still suffered seasonal mood changes and maniacal blips, but I managed to stay in control.

I felt wanted by the children who enjoyed my activities. My sons felt pushed out. – at times, I was obsessively dedicated to the children of the village to keep my sanity. I enjoyed that period immensely. My 'me' time.

People of the village who had previously avoided the local 'mad' woman were now praising her for her community efforts. I had proven myself worthy in society. Sometimes you must step back and work harder at a giant leap forward, to avoid the bipolar isolated traps you can fall into.

I am proud of my achievements of creative entertainment for children in my village of birth. This was the stepping stone of moving forward, sanely. Bipolar doesn't leave you, but you can learn to liaise with it, and live with it, and be functional.

Eventually my marriage broke down. We couldn't find the love we had before. I believe the deep love hadn't been there in the first place. We had got together too young and naïve, and for the wrong reasons. When things became progressively difficult for us as a couple, the air pressure within our home started to cave in on our relationship. The air you breathe stifles you when the environment is intense and unrepairable. I felt ill physically, and so did my husband.

If one partner is unco-operative when it comes to receiving counselling therapy, then the other doesn't know what to do other than save their own health. A bad relationship wrecks your personal health and the children suffer in bad tensions. Husband didn't go to marriage counselling with me. I went alone. He didn't even read the pamphlets of support I brought home. I called time on him. I told my sons I wanted to leave their father. They told me to go if I felt that way and they stayed with their father. I left in the clothes I stood in. I wasn't going to risk bipolar becoming more aggressive through poor relationship issues. I left the scout movement. I left him. I gained my freedom.

I only had God and prayer to get me through the wrecking ball of emotional divorce stress, and I am glad I have always had a deep spiritual interest in all cultures, religions and faiths. I have absorbed a multitude of comforting blessings from many spiritually diverse people who have crossed my childhood and adult life and prayed with me over the years to release the demon thoughts I held within and supported me in difficult times. I thank these people silently. Regularly. They will all hold a special place in my soul forever. Whether I see these people or never see them again, they stay in my life, in my heart, and gain my love eternally. The power of humble spirituality is an enormous benefit for positive energy.

The positive energy forces of life will always overpower negative destructive sources. We can stand united in this and believe that mass belief in spiritual power will defeat those who cause physical pain and death.

Stay in control of your mind. Losing it only loses a life.

Second Chance

I was working in five jobs to make ends meet. I met someone to love. I felt the same drawn feelings as I had with ex-husband. I felt it was meant to be. He was totally different to my ex. He was tall, broad, looked very rough and rugged. He had a different outlook on life, and heavy social habits. I moved in with him quickly and bred three children with him.

Unfortunately, as much as I thought he would settle down to a quiet happy life with me, he didn't. He seemed to have his own head of psychotic thoughts. He drank too much alcohol and talked foolishly and unkindly through it, claiming the next morning that he couldn't remember anything. I really don't know why I never moved on; this blasé attitude of drunken forgetfulness was unforgivably too repetitive. I gained some income from the sale of a previous home and I could have moved out, with my first-born girl – whom he fathered – and left him. I didn't. I made the best out of the relationship.

I cared for him deep inside and I wanted to rescue his social binging. He found it hard to live with the responsibilities of raising a family. He chose to spend many weekends in the pub rather than stay at home or take us out. I gained very irritable thoughts and started to shout and swear a lot. I felt totally aggressive, tired and frustrated with life. I moved in with a man I barely knew and I often felt if I had half of him and half of the ex-husband, I would have created the good qualities out of both, into a bespoke man for myself.

Two years after my daughter's birth came another son. The nice thing about having more children, is that it brought my adult sons back into my life. They seemed genuinely pleased to have more siblings.

The father of my young children was so unpredictable in character. Sometimes he was happy and generous and sometimes selfish and intoxicated. I found it difficult to be tactile with him when he was sober – he seemed to have a barrier – but when we went out socially, he relaxed and seemed more loving and tactile. The drink was his mask. Sometimes I thought he just didn't like life unless he was drunk.

I knew in my heart our future life wasn't workable as a couple together. I was lucky that I suffered more physical ill health than poor mental health carrying our three children. My maturity and long gap between two lots of families helped to stop the mental illness manifesting. I loved my children and they kept me busy with chores. My partner was hurtful, and mentally and physically abusive; he hated parting with money for the children and myself. He was a fearful man. He'd turn a key in the door late at night and play a Russian roulette of mad moods with me. I never knew how he'd react each time he came home. He'd roll into bed, reeking of beer and fag breath, groping me and muttering how much he loved me. Other occasions he'd prod me awake and moan rubbish repetitively with anger. He petrified my heart. I felt emotionally insecure, vulnerable and sad. I just wanted a normal happy loving man, not a body of abuse through beer.

Whether he earned his drinking money or not, no one has the right to make their partners or children unhappy and in fear, through their own selfish intoxication.

My partner's mother died when our son was a baby, which worsened his drinking and his moods. He caused problems at the funeral 'wake' and this encouraged me to think about the future. I was scared how volatile he was. I was disappointed he needed to drink till he was incoherent. I didn't want this sort of life with a young family. I imagined my children to be raised in a pub; it seemed as if it was the only way they would see him in the future. My personality didn't help and I gained an aggressive tone in my voice, which irritated him. Sometimes he would manhandle me through drink. A slap on the face, a push, and he threw me out on the street with my babies a few times. The life was unstable. I didn't develop maniacal tendencies at the beginning. My life was full of baby routines. We gained a third child, another girl, so my days were full of nappies with pre-school children.

We couldn't make each other happy. I hoped he was the one I would share the rest of my life with, but he wasn't. He seemed crazier than me in his head thoughts. There wasn't room for two of us to be crazy. I felt that it was best to try to move on, but it's difficult when you have nowhere to go. A friend offered me a rented property in the north. I was tempted to take it, but my heart felt I had to try and make things work. I declined it.

I struggled in the uneasy air. I struggled to be a mum. He wasn't hands on to help me much. I appreciated his nieces visiting and staying for holidays. They helped me a lot. One of the nieces wasn't happy with her own home life, she was a great support. We had some good girly times together, and I did lean on her a lot to help me. I was constantly mentally exhausted. I suffered a lot of bipolar lows in the eight years I lived with my partner. I lost my bubbliness, my enthusiasm for life and my creativeness. More importantly, I lost myself as a person. Where I had gained a decent sex-life and social life, I had lost a stable family secure feeling, and my personality and self-esteem had perished. I never felt I belonged with the children's father.

I felt he was just passing through my life and it was meant to be like that. I was meant to be a mother of his three children. I was meant to meet the fathers of my children. These were all meant to be events in my life.

My life was mapped out. My life was meant to be challenging. I was meant to conquer. The purpose of existence was to accept what was thrown at me and live through it. I was meant to be *superwoman*. I wasn't. I was a broken woman and a sad hurt woman.

Mother's Premonition

My mother said that she dreamt of a tall broad man with dark hair, brown eyes. He was walking along a road with a blonde girl with brown eyes. She told me he would be my second partner. She told me when my elder sons were only two and four years old and my marriage to blonde-haired husband was still young. She told me three months before she died. I laughed at the time. She told my sister-in-law the dream. My mother felt she was dying. She gave me a birthday card a month before she died. My birthday was three months after her death. Why prepare a card so early? She knew she was dying, and she knew my life would change in the future. My life changed 15 years after her death, so Mother was gifted to have prophesised my changes of lifestyle. Aunty felt her own death too. Aunty had promised to take me to see her workplace. Aunty told me the day would never come, she knew she was slipping away. We were special people. Mother, Aunty and I. We sensed death. Our senses could feel a soul slip away from the body. We could feel events happening for others if we enlightened our senses further.

Extra Sensory Perception (ESP)

People who are not aware of psychic nature don't understand the people who make use of their extra sensory gifts. Emotions are highly strung or magnified because it's part of a person's genetic make-up. The person who has ESP must channel this energy into being functional. If the energy isn't channelled, then a mixed-up head occurs and a person becomes fantasised into a state of oblivion, unusual thoughts and potential madness. This is not a problem for a GP or even a psychiatrist because neither can offer support for a person who has exceptional high senses.

The person must appear threatening to their own health, or someone else's health, before the medical authorities intervene, and the only support they can receive is tranquillisation of the person whose senses are heightened. This is because doctors don't understand ESP emotions enough to find a different way, and chemical companies govern the health services and their methods of treating people. People who are gifted have choices: either to ignore their gifts and struggle to control their emotions or make use of their gifts to benefit themselves and others and embrace that they are gifted.

Psychic people are not mental, nor freaks, but very special gifted people with special emotions.

Mind Pictures and Surreal Movement

My mind has been enhanced to a higher level.

When I close my eyes, I see coloured visions of faces and scenarios, and a lot of purple and yellow colours. When I close my eyes I can move my arms without moving them, my spirit arms move the invisible ones. A strange feeling to be lying peacefully, but not quite in slumber, and thinking the arm is stretching outwards but it's still in the same position. I never used to visualise in colour; it used to be just greys and black. I think I would find it easy to open my third eye. I did try to chill to third eye music sounds, but it felt surreal to raise myself to a higher dimension so I stopped doing it. I do crush my abilities. I worry I will go insane, or witness things that would upset me.

I don't want to lose control over my senses.

Violence

I adored my three young children's grandparents. His mother reminded me of my aunty. His father was a jovial man. I really did like them both. They were humble people, kind and down-to-earth. I will never know how they could have bred a man like him. He was bitter on the inside. His parents were nice people. They both died prematurely. Sad for my children to lose grandparents.

I had to leave him. He beat my eyes to a racoon circled bruised pulp. He beat me so aggressively my elder daughter woke up screaming in my terrifying moment. I said the Lord's prayer and Hail Mary silently. I expected to die at his hands, as he was intoxicated. I truly felt he would kill me in that moment in time. Thank God I shut my eyes as the force of his beating could have wrecked my eye nerves. A black shadow square blanked my mind. I am sure in that moment of time, that even the angel of death wanted to shelter me. I wasn't a bad woman and he painted me bad. He believed rubbish talk in the pub that I had an affair with a man from the pub. I hadn't. I wouldn't have dared. I was too scared of him. I wouldn't have wanted to anyway, I wanted *him*, no one else. I was constantly exhausted from looking after the kids.

When a man drinks too much, he doesn't know what he says. He looks a fool. He changes like Jekyll and Hyde, he acts unintelligently. He listens to other sad fools who are unhappy in life, his senses robbed.

I am a bonding woman. I form a relationship and I hang on to it like a leech. I will only let go if I get beaten and trodden on. Once you are down the only way is up. Social binge-drinking encourages madness of speech, it's not pleasant to listen to, it irritates me, I feel that it's dumb. I have no time for dumb sounding drunken people. My eyes are my most precious asset. I wasn't going to risk a beating like that again.

He gave me six months to leave his property. I left in five. I needed to find myself again with a young family in tow. I was prepared to be a single parent and bring up the children myself. I couldn't lead a life of living in fear. The children would have a more normal life if we were left alone to cope. We left.

I gave my children a better life by raising them on my own. They have done things they wouldn't have been able to because of his greed and need for drink.

I made the right decision to move on.

"Power to Womanhood!"

Move forward, stay strong. The only way is onward and forward and not turning back to repeat the same circle.

Ghosts Do Exist

I sense noises that are ghostly. The house I lived in with my ex second partner had a ghost of a boy. He used to run up and down the landing. I would hear the running with my bedroom door open wide. There was no one there, just a running noise. A person would have had to cross my bedroom door frame, but no one did; just running noises of the feet.

My elder daughter was three when she moved into this house. On the first night of sleeping in her own bedroom she said a boy was sat behind me while I was reading her a bedtime story. I put it down to the new environment upsetting her. There was no one there when I turned around. I did feel coldness on my back, but that was all.

I found out from local people that a young boy a long time ago had got killed running after his ball down the back of the alley of our house. He had run into a lorry at the bottom of the alley. The ghost boy never hurt us. He just ran across the landing every night. My eldest son heard the noise too. He had moved in with us and heard the noise when we chatted one night after he finished work. He investigated and realised that it wasn't the young kids. I was sad to leave the house when I left the children's father. I liked the house.

I got used to the ghost too.

In my present home I hear things too. Sometimes the lights switch off by themselves. My daughters feel a presence too and sometimes a shadow man appears, but we all learn to live with it. The ghostly phenomena don't bother us enough to do something about it.

If you live with the noises peacefully, a ghost will stay peaceful.

Ghosts are only troubled if people are troubled.

I have seen a ghost of a Victorian lady. She is supposed to be a ghost of a local pub. I know she is a ghost because she hasn't any feet, and she's a translucent apparition. I've seen her on the bridge near my home. I went to the pub she haunts.

The toilet door flung open out of the blue one night, and there were footsteps in the toilet, and someone went in next cubicle, but when I came out of the toilet the next cubicle was empty and wide open and no one had left the toilet room. There were only two cubicles. I was the only one in there.

This has happened several times. I tell the ghosts to calm down. I have learnt to live with phenomena. I have learnt to live with the 'other side'. I believe we have three worlds, and we live in different dimensions. We are all individuals. People think we are in the same time gap as each other.

I know we live in our own space with an energy barrier. We live in our own pockets of time.

A person passing by on a street could be seconds forward or backwards.

Who knows what time and space are?

Scientists only work out reason; spiritual reason is not in their equation.

Single-life Bipolar Parent – New Start

"We are going on holiday," I said to the children in the taxi. We were travelling to our new home with a dog, a cat and a tank full of fish in tow. I didn't tell the ex I was leaving him. I didn't trust his temperament. He might have turned on me if he was threatened with losing his kids. My young son guessed we were in the town we frequently visited. He recognised the place; it wasn't a holiday. We arrived at our new home and we group hugged in a bare room. I felt relieved I had personal space. I felt distraught and felt that I had failed again in a relationship and failed my children. I needed to assess my future life.

The stress of the move was phenomenal. The secrecy behind it burdened my heart so much. I was blessed with good friends who helped me move. I could not have moved on without them. I will eternally be grateful for the love and the time and the effort they put in to help me ease into a better life. I know they are special people in my life. I feel blessed to have the friends I have. I couldn't ask my brothers to support me. This was the second disastrous relationship that involved children. My brothers believed in staying together and riding over the problems and working things out.

My relationships were impossible to work out, my sanity was more important. The children needed me more than they needed their dad. I truly believed that if I had stayed in a volatile relationship based on drinking as a priority, I would have ended up dead or the children would have had little stimulation for growing up in a decent life. Greed and selfishness go hand in hand when alcohol is in someone's blood. This wasn't my upbringing. Polish people are great drinkers, but there was control in our family line and family values and family priority came first.

Most Polish people drink at home, with family and friends they like, and keep a happy atmosphere.

Pub drinkers drink with people who are acquaintances, and social binging drinkers get drunk and talk foolishly and get aggravated. Drink changes the character. I would always have had to sing for my supper, and the kids too, if I had stayed with him, as he was too selfish as a person to part with the amount of money really needed to bring up the children. I had a hands-on ex-husband before him, who put all his money on the table, doted on his kids, and always provided with no quibble. I got it wrong again.

Man couldn't please me or my bipolar. Man wrecked my health and used me. Man chiselled deep wounds in my heart and diminished my self-worth. The only way forward was to bring up the children alone, even if I must live in rags and put my personal relationship life on hold. I know I did the right thing. The stress of the move flipped me into mania and I tipped over into insanity once more.

The father moved into my new home to look after his children, as I still let him have parental access rights. I'm not a mean mother, problems were between us; his relationship with his children was fine. I ventured into a hallucinated time and mended again in hospital. This time I thought I could jump as high as the moon; I was counting lift off in my head. I must have thought I was a space shuttle. Natural bouncing highs became chaotically disorganised.

The old Victorian hospital building was closed. I was entering a different care unit in another hospital.

New building, new environment, new patients, new madness scenarios, and another haunting worry of doubts, nervous feelings with apprehensive unsettling thoughts. I hadn't been inside for 16 years. It was the last time I was admitted. I never went back again, and I never want to.

I was stronger, I came to my senses quicker, I was more aware of my surroundings and I felt I didn't belong to a psychiatric unit any more. A psychiatric stay was not relevant for me and unhelpful to heal me. I seemed to be an advisor to everyone else, propping up sick patients' madness and making sure the medical students learnt enough knowledge.

Care in the community was the way forward for me, and I received excellent community nursing care.

I feel blessed and lucky to have lived in Charnwood, to have the doctors and community nurse care. I consider these people to be part of my soul forever, as they are genuinely understanding and encouraging.

My angel support workers.

I learned to snap out of any psychotic tendencies quickly within a couple of days. I stayed in hospital for three weeks. I should have stayed longer but the children's father demanded the hospital release me; he wasn't going to care for the children any longer, he needed to work. Most people would question why the father didn't bring up the children himself and become their guardian, because the mother was prone to losing her sanity.

This wasn't going to happen; he was too selfish and too tight with his money and too flippant to be a good father and mother to his children.

I found it hard to find another relationship because three young children are overpowering. No one wants the responsibility of bringing up other people's kids. Some people do find happiness with someone else who takes their children on board, but no one wanted to take my bipolar on board, so I struggled to raise the kids for many years, with vicious mood head swings in-between mad blip moments, which wasn't kind for the children.

The children learnt quickly how to react to my ill health.

I am a difficult mother, but I am grateful my children coped admirably with my illness and have loved me unconditionally however I have behaved. They are now old enough to lead their own lives and I feel I have managed to bring them up quite well amongst my mental health problems.

I know I am not alone in my position as a single parent but to have an illness such as bipolar, with ADHD too, and with a volatile loud character, I felt I had a task to keep my moods under control. Life was so lonely for me as an adult. My bipolar feeds off the sex drive. It savours intimacy, closeness, warmth, heat, love and touch.

If I didn't have a man in my life, I was nasty, I was angry, I was tetchy, I was a volcano – I became my father.

The same crazy impulsive, unpredictable outbursts.

My childhood past finally clicked. Father was crazy because Mother never kept him happy. I felt crazy if I didn't have a lover. High bipolar craves a sex life. Without a sex life my mind goes berserk with random thoughts of wanting to hurt. My father exercised control over his madness and didn't behave as maniacally as I did. Maybe that was because he worked all his life and didn't have a clue how to bring kids up – my mother was responsible for our upbringing. I screamed my way through disciplining the kids. Maybe this was inappropriate at times, but I had to let the anger out by having a tantrum, by 'going on one'. This was the only way to stamp out the stresses, and any thoughts of hurting physically. Bringing up children and being totally responsible as one parent is so hard. Having bipolar too as part of the set-up, made life ten times harder. Bipolar is destructive. A rage can turn into a blind kill. I never let the blind rages get that far.

My eldest daughter summed up the feelings of how life with a bipolar mum is when she shared with me how she felt as she grew up in my care: The environment was scary when a young child, then it became irritating as a primary child, then it became anger-making for her as a young teenager. She had to learn when to stay quiet and disappear out of the way.

Now daughter is an adult, my outbursts have become irritating once more, but she says she always feels loved and secure. This is good to hear. My child still feels secure. She is old enough now to understand that this is how mother is. She lives with it. I felt secure in my family home too when witnessing my father's behaviour.

I feel I have done my best to disperse evil negative thoughts of hurting. I know I have brought my children up as best as I could hope for. I am still here today, where others have let go and moved on spiritually into the unknown after-life.

Psychotic bipolar does make me feel I want to cause pain to others, but my heart is good, and I sidetrack the negative thoughts often. Spiritual strength works for me. Prayer does wonders. Having a religious upbringing helps me to stay focused.

Shouting can be hurtful, it can be mentally stressful to others, but it was the only way I could get the anger in me to dispel. I was glad that I balanced the angry mood swings with spending quality time with the kids.

Life has not been easy for my offspring, but children are quick to understand signs of a storm brewing, just like I had to with my father.

I never leant on heavy social vices to blot out the bipolar swings. I have 'stayed in control', without leaning on drink or street drugs.

I have always been aware of my family responsibilities as a single parent. I only drank alcohol to chill, not to get drunk. The same life is still there if you try to blot things out, and the only way to move forward is to realise what the illness is all about, see the signs, and tackle the negative feelings. I love my family line enough to ride the storms. I am lucky. I was born into a family who love me, and I love them, even if they don't understand me and feel useless to help me. Spiritual bonding in a family line is an unseen force of the deepest love, even though we all live separate lives and function independently of each other. I am still here *alive* to write my life story.

How Do Bipolar Swings Feel?

When I was in my 20s my mind was still maturing so bipolar totally upset my train of thoughts and ran away with me. I couldn't grasp what was happening, I was like a train derailing, a plane falling out of the sky, a boat sinking, and a car crashing; all these sensations in one mad moment. Then the sex drive revved up when I was prone to feeling high, so I felt like a motorbike revving up, and jumping over ramps like a dare devil stuntman. The sex drive is an incredible energy force when prone to mania highs; it sends confusing messages to the brain and it makes me run around like a headless chicken.

My two sons by first husband missed out on reading with mother at bedtime and having creative time with me like drawing and making things and playing board games.

I spent a lot of time in and out of hospital as my head spun out of control and orbited into self-oblivion, so I lost a lot of years in rearing and loving my first two sons and they must have felt this loss during their childhood.

I was mum to them, mood blips inclusive. The boys had great supportive grandparents and a supportive father.

I am thankful they had carers they knew and loved.

The three children from second partner received a lot of my time as I was raising them without a husband. We couldn't afford to do much outside the home as they grew, so I made sure I created games to play, and arts and craft to do, and encouraged other children who lived on our street to come and play too.

I was Mother Hubbard with tons of kids in my cupboard. The house is well worn and loved these days.

When the children were old enough to take up hobbies, I burned my high energy by taking them to after school activities.

I didn't drive so walked a lot. The best way to curb the waves of unsettled bipolar moods is to channel energy in functional positive ways, mentally and physically. I hope my children feel that there were parts of their life that were fun with me. I hope my children's friends who have grown with mine feel the same too. I did well to channel my excessive crazy energy.

My bark is not a bite, but my mind can be explosive and unkind, I can be unpredictable in my actions.

The only regret I have is that bipolar encouraged *swearing*. I cannot control my tongue although I do swear less now. Everything that gets on top of me in life is matched with poor, colourful language.

The surprise is that none of my five children have grown up with repetitive swearing. They only swear when they are extremely angry. I guess they used to get tired of hearing me, I swore enough for them all. Thankfully.

I am so blessed to have had my children; they all love me, and they all realise I have been plagued with bipolar, and I feel they all have had to grow up so fast in childhood to cope with having an unstable mum. I love my children so much. They know this. I am glad I have them in my life. I hope they stay healthy and have fruitful happy long lives.

Bipolar creates difficulties. Difficulties in dealing with paperwork, such as forms to fill in, school letters to read, appointments to keep, and realising sense of time and routine. Sometimes even a difficult situation unexpectedly occurring can send me in a flap. I make mountains because I can only see mountains, so even if the problem is resolvable it doesn't seem so to me.

When in a state of high or low, sometimes errors of judgement can be made, like stepping in front of traffic, not knowing sense of direction. Domestic home chores can seem too great a workload, and a dinner can be difficult to cook. When I have felt life has been too much in one day, I don't do anything the next day other than lie down and listen to music on the radio or music in my phone.

Sometimes it's best to forsake an appointment, give up a chore, leave the paperwork if feeling burdened. Excess pressure is not worth losing my head over. I avoid situations that set off panic attacks and fantasies, and push myself to stay in control of reality by focusing on things that make me feel good and relaxed.

I met and welcomed a few lovers.

I wanted a man, I wanted a fulfilling sex life, and I was lucky to have a pretty face to be able to draw a man into my life. More than one, during my single parenthood life. Some men feel overpowered by me, I am too much in the face. Others are fascinated by me, but whatever the outcome I give a damn good ride. I am loving and sensual, wild and sexy, and my eyes can mesmerise in sex play. I am one spider's web where a 'man fly' would love to be caught.

I can be obsessive, possessive, and jealous too. Some men find those traits a 'turn on' by making them feel needed; others can run a mile.

Bipolar is a wrecking ball for relationships and a partner must be special to have the ability to weather all storms of moods, to walk alongside me.

I can make a man feel sexually heightened and his self-esteem feel great.

He can feel wanted and loved and fulfilled or I can pain his heart in loud temper tantrums, so he is hurt and runs away. My attitude towards a man depends on whether he can ride out my erratic mood waves and whether he has shown a sad side to his nature like dishonesty, disloyalty, by taking me for granted or feeding lies to my face. I cannot stand lies.

I can make a man feel loved even in conversation alone. Long term I can be destructive, erratic and seem uncaring and obsessed. When men haven't made me happy, my relationships have dissolved. I don't think I can live with a man again, I will constantly feel suffocated; and I always walk a wilderness path alone in body and my thoughts.

I never join people's circles. People must scale my barrier to enter mine. I always feel isolated, and I feel that people should want to be in my life and find me, and not for me to find them. My soul draws people into my life, not my looks. I am grateful for the few friendships and acquaintances I have gained; they are special people in my lifetime.

I believe that God is drifting amongst people. I believe that people are drawn together by unknown spiritual forces and our paths are fated to meet and mingle with each other.

We are written in the stars. I also feel that freak accidents and some illnesses are created by bad negativity stirring them.

Too much negative electrical energy in an area can cause mass destruction either through weather or unfortunate events happening to all living things. Therefore it's important to all humans to unite and give out well-being vibes and not inflict negativity on others. Raising spiritual well-being to higher levels will benefit our soul when it moves on in death as a wave of energy current.

I have written a poem about light. All my poetry is written from the deepest part of my soul.

LIGHT

There is light at the end of darkness.
There is light in living too,
the spiritual unknown that awaits us
shines light from sun, stars, and moon.
There is light in every lightning strike,
because negative energies fall somewhere.
Good light shines when vibes are lifted
when well-being is collectively shared.
There are many problems bestowed upon us,
it's easy to not see the light,
so warm your soul to shine,
an everlasting light that's bright.
If everyone feels each other's positive energy
The light will shine strong,
But if darkness overcomes a person,
the feeling will be gloomy and wrong.
If you let negativity overcast you,
it will cause suffering, isolation and despair.
Don't let the dark light take a grip,
don't let it torment you inside.
Find a path to walk in the light,
and let light be your guide.

SHINE A SOULFUL LIGHT.
LOVE AND PEACE TO ALL.

Conclusion

I have lived a life of turmoil, and I have shown many sides to my character. The empath feelings within me are so incredibly absorbing of everyone and everything I witness and live through. Therefore I can react badly, but happily too. I truly believe I am a sponge that draws life's problems in as a receiver, and that's why I spit and shout – but equally I act humbly, generously, selflessly when I see kindness, loving and care.

My eyes are a witness from the unknown realm, and I am a time traveller of many forms. I was born to this Earth to pave the way for future change. What sort of change I really don't know, until I comatose and shed my skin, and onward to the unknown I go.

My life has begun a new phase.

I have tumbled, I have tossed, I have loved and lost.

I have fought insanity.

Ignorance must fade to enlighten hope, for those who are mentally ill and can't cope.

Everyone can succumb to thoughts of gloom, so fight the mind and help it bloom creatively.

Please shine thoughts of love, faith, dreams and good deed; don't give up on the world when you are in need. You can get better, *you* can change your mind thoughts and lifestyle.

I did.

I was lost in an oblivious madness a very long while. I am still struggling with my mind waves but **I STAY STRONG**.

You stay strong too please, and shine your inner soul with light.

Love, Light and Blessings.

A quote from Sigmund Freud:

"Out of your vulnerabilities will come your strength"

Everyone is beautiful in God's presence.

So, let the beauty shine from within your soul, to encourage the strength of a positive mind, and a future worthwhile goal in life and after death.

Kate Dobrowolska

STAY IN CONTROL with a peaceful healthy spirit.

A spiritual thought of long past
In memory of my table tennis friend
Wendy, who chose to fall too soon,
but will never be forgotten in my heart.

PETAL WITHIN A NETTLE

Kate Dobrowolska

Introduction

The illness I suffer, bipolar 1 disorder, contributes to damaging personal relationships. People who have bipolar high tendencies can become promiscuous to feed a sexual buzz or have several relationships because they are difficult to be with. The title for this second part of my life story has a double meaning in the word 'nettle'. A nettle can be a stinging plant, and nettle can also mean 'one who enjoys the company of men for sexual reasons'. In this second part I describe my sexual relationships, and the difficulties I have to maintain happiness within them. I aim to describe the feelings of a bipolar head when interacting with a man in a relationship. I will also describe how my illness affects people who love me. I was born to be challenged, and people are challenged to know me. I am emotionally high maintenance. I am difficult to please. Vocally I appear to be judgemental, but I see myself as opinionated.

I am highly emotionally charged. I exude a feeling of well-being with a man I fall for. An acquaintance said to me, that I made his heart and soul feel warm every time he saw me cross his path. For the right man I am the right woman. I just seem to take a lot of wrong turns.

Sigmund Freud said:

"The sexual life of adult women is a dark continent for psychology."

Maybe he should have met me. I might have shown him some light.

Kate Dobrowolska

First Love

> *"Women are like apples on trees. The best ones are at the top of the tree. Most men don't want to reach for the good ones, because they are afraid of falling and getting hurt. Instead they just take the rotten apples from the ground that aren't as good but easy. The apples at the top think something is wrong with them, when, they are amazing. They just have to wait for the right man to come along, the one who's brave enough to climb all the way to the top of the tree."*
>
> **Sigmund Freud**

I was a rosy, shiny, scrumptious looking apple at 16 years old. Pure, unblemished, shining and mouth-watering. Sat on top of the tree like an angel on a Christmas tree. I met Thomas. My first love. My knight in shining armour. He was chivalrous and smart. He was fit and adventurous and climbed to the top of the tree to take that first bite of me. Sadly, I was a poisoned apple; I poisoned his soul with erratic sexual mood swings – *and he spat me out.*

16 years of age and not emotionally mature enough to understand how a girl should feel over a man. Hormones scattered in different directions in my body. Impulsive, stroppy, naïve and sheltered. I made a decision about commitment based on the striking blueness of his eyes, his beautiful smile and humble personality. I somehow forgot to realise that to fall in love, you went weak at the knees, and felt butterflies, and longed to see a true love again. He in turn was bowled over by my feistiness, my unpredictable changing character, and my enthusiasm for passion and tactile touching.

When we decided to marry in the month of April in 1979 we attended three sessions of spiritual Christian education with my local priest.

The Catholic priest explained the sanctity of marriage and the relation of God to people and people to each other. The priest said electricity was the main key to happiness. We looked at each other with a puzzled expression, such was our ignorance of what real sexual attraction was about and how magnetising a compatible sexual nature could be. The main struggle in our marriage was the incompatibility of our sex drives.

We were complete opposites in needing affection and sexual interaction. I was raring to stoke his fire and consume him with burning passion. He seemed to want to be a cold fish settled at the bottom of the sea floor avoiding the shark's insatiable appetite. The shark was I. We struggled throughout our marriage with his lack of sexual need. He hadn't any regular desires; just the occasional need once a month.

Thomas was content as the giver of provisions – the hunter who made sure his woman and children were well cared for. He seemed to lack the ability to be tactile and affectionate. His head was so methodical and structured with strategical precision. I was fiery, temperamental, explosively lush. I felt needy constantly, my petal itched for impregnation. My breasts heaved for a caress. I didn't understand personal space barriers – I didn't realise at such a young age. He had a huge invisible barrier surrounding him. He seemed to be a genie in a bottle, but I didn't know what command to use to make my sexual desires come true.

I wondered why I wasn't enough for sexual loving in abundance. I was pretty at 17 years old. My body was average and curvy in my youth.

Thomas's sex drive was low and mine was high but his stubbornness to not improve our relationship was sad. Thomas was four years older than me. He should have known that a pretty young Polish girl, genetically inflamed, would want to be worshipped sexually like a goddess.

Thomas didn't think it was a problem. It was.

I suffered, I suffered physically, I suffered mentally, I inherited bipolar early in life. A trigger of energy in childbirth put my mind into a fast-paced orbit of sexual frenzy which confused my head into becoming mentally ill. When I was diagnosed as a manic depressive, my psychiatrist Dr K, told me that I had the wrong partner to help me cope with my sexual nature. My husband Thomas showed him hands on qualities of being a good father and a good loyal husband and provider, but my illness was a sexual infestation of extreme needy desires that caused anger, mind torment and unworthy feelings if not fulfilled.

I suspect my psychiatrist felt that Thomas was passionless, and he was astute in his assessment of our marital relationship. The bipolar cravings of sexual lust were suffocated by Thomas's lack of sexual need. My high needs were crushing my soul slowly into a painful compressed gnawed state. Manic depression is bipolar disorder – they are both the same illness.

When you are in your early 20s, you are still maturing; you are still learning how to have self-control, how to stop raging hormones running away from you, and a mental illness is an added burden. It is easy to be obsessed by your own body functions going haywire, so you don't even notice your partner is behaving just as crazy in another way, struggling with his immature issues as a young adult. Invisible barriers build around your body and it's hard to reach each other to understand each other. I used to focus a lot on Thomas's eyes, and his eyes were striking sky blue and angelic. I sometimes felt he wasn't a human. He was an angel in disguise guiding me, protecting me, a buffer for my mental anguish. He was tormented though; he felt unloved by his mother who seemed to dote on her daughter, his older sister, more than on him.

The unloving rejection from him paved the way for me to suffer my mental anxieties because he pushed me away a lot and he wasn't a tactile man. I suffered severe frustration, throughout the 19-year marriage. I blame myself for our rocky relationship. I seem to be tactile at the beginning of a relationship, then expect the man to take over and worship my body and soul.

Thomas wasn't the sort of man to make first advances, so we got nowhere with this attitude. Looking back at our relationship, there were never enough hugs and kisses between us. We were just performing repetitive daily actions like a chore. I felt that we were thrown together to make the best out of each day. Thomas was a flirt which made me feel insecure. I wanted him to have only eyes for me, but we constantly had an invisible shield between us, and he had an annoying habit of sweet-talking women who crossed our path. He even helped them out with chores they needed doing.

With me, he wasn't passionate and had no heat in his body. He was aloof, and lovemaking was like a needy action – mechanical – rather than passionate and ensuing out of desire.

I, in return, couldn't feel passion for him. He didn't make my heart beat fast, he didn't turn my petal into a burning bush. I didn't know how to tell him verbally if I felt sexy out of the blue. He rejected my advances in bed so many times that I developed a complex of rejection which irritated my body. I used to suffer dense feelings by myself in tears. My stomach would clench me in a hard grip, gnawing me, tickling me, making me feel sick.

I drank wine at home regularly to make myself feel tired, and strangely Thomas seemed to get aroused if I was tipsy. I am sure his prowess was exhilarated with power because he felt more confident to be in control of the sexual situation when I was drunk.

The relationship between Thomas and myself was strange when I started having psychotic bipolar attacks. Looking at him through psychosis, he seemed to adopt a robotic body through my eyes. He looked stiff and moved in a sequence of timing that didn't suit my vision. He breathed heavily; I could feel his energy trying to control his anxiety and I became scared of him. Bipolar makes you feel vulnerable and scared by everyone. I used to run upstairs and hide under the duvet and hope my wild crazy state would disappear in slumber. Thomas wasn't a physically aggressive man, but the tension of high feelings brought on my fearful emotions. I believe the energy waves we exude can adversely affect reactions from our partners.

I believe Thomas found it difficult to be responsible for my sexual ill health, so when I became mentally unstable, he became annoyed and felt I was a burden. So it was hardly a loving approach, considering I was the love of his life, his wife.

Thomas stopped fancying me as soon as the mental health pills increased my weight.

In the early years of our marriage, I had many trials of different medication. At one point I was taking between 15 and 20 pills a day just to control the insanity. The more pills the doctors gave me the more my mind and body wanted to reject and become resilient, and the weight piled on in two months. The pills affected the hormones that controlled weight, because a lot of the time while in an oblivious state I didn't eat properly or in quantity.

Lovemaking with Thomas was humdrum. Just like people having a set dinner pattern – sausage and mash on Mondays, eggs and chips Tuesdays, roast dinner Sundays – sex between us was the same. Missionary position Mondays, me on top Tuesdays, and a suck of the nob Sundays, except the days of the week were not consecutive. Monday was one month, and Tuesday was the following month, and the 39 days in between hurt my petal to a withered state.

Bipolar craves imaginative stimulation when going through a high state; if sexual interest isn't matched, the nerves in the body pulsate bruised and itchy. This in turn feeds the brain with negative thoughts of anger, frustration, irritability and severe black depressive spells. There seems to be a distinct gap in the brain where thought patterns lose control, and the mouth spits out obscenities and vulgar talk that upsets people. My bipolar is extremely volatile.

When I am in the mood for intimacy and want to experience the desired intimate feelings I crave, I crave more when the power of ecstatic orgasm has subsided; it revs up more. The petal is itching again within minutes, thus exploding repetitive desires for continual consecutive performance or volatile deathly anger thoughts occur, and my body performs actions maniacally.

I have never heard of a metal phallic organ transplant in man to absorb a bipolar woman's disordered desires, which can run on an ever-ready battery power. I cannot win. I cannot be kept on a happy chemical equilibrium. I have pushed men away with such a strong wind force and become isolated and alone again. Time and time again.

Thomas, my first love, was an exceptional family man and a good provider. He grafted hard in a job, but he suffered his own anxieties that were pushing me away. A fetish I couldn't deal with. Ten years into our marriage I found out the reason why Thomas never expelled his sexual energy on me. He felt more comfortable in play imagination and visual stimulation by other sources. He was far happier entertaining himself, and that didn't bode well for my strong, high, tactile. physical needs all of which were crippling my sexual emotions. Our marriage fell apart in the end because I became very fat and unkempt and struggled with my mental health continually; Thomas became more and more unhappy and more mentally abusive and distant. We parted after 19 years of marriage.

We were both scout leaders in the late 1980s, up to the mid-1990s and we substituted passion for each other for the goal of developing a flourishing scout group. When we decided to leave the scout group, we found that we had nothing in common, other than our pets and arguing all the time. I will always have a little love in my heart for Thomas – he was my first love – but I decided to move on to find my happiness because he never made me happy, and he made me feel very mentally ill.

I moved out of his life hoping I would walk into something more exciting and rewarding. I walked into something excitingly dangerous. I walked into HELL – and my second partner's drinking issues.

Second Partner Abuse

Stewart walked into the pub. Larger than life, intimidating, brutish. I sensed sadness in his soul and a deep vacated hole. My veins stirred as if embracing a round in a boxing ring. Curiosity. Wildness. Excitement. Fear and wonder pulsated around my body. My heart beat fast, the air around me magnetised him to me. He thought I was gorgeous. I spoke to him and we exchanged ritual pleasantries. He seemed aloof, his barrier was huge, he was unapproachable, but the challenge inside me persisted to chase. The second time we bumped into each other in the pub, he noticed I was attracted to him. He approached me and asked me why I didn't notice his eyes. Eyes? I hadn't noticed anything unusual. His aura was placed in front of me and he was the pursuit. He told me he had had countless operations, that he had been bullied as a child over his eyes. I wasn't concerned, he was meant to be. I was meant to be in his life.

We became pub friends. Drinking together, no intimacy, just friends. Nine months later he took me out for a meal. I looked at him and said I was going to have his child. I said this out of the blue, we hadn't even been heavily intimate. Just a kiss and a cuddle. Something deep inside me told me he was the one. I had to go with the flow of the airwaves.

I moved in with Stewart two weeks before Christmas. My relationship with Thomas had suffocated. It was resting in the grave. No resurrection was possible. 19 years of marriage crumbled to dust.

I should have known it would be a disaster. I found Stewart difficult to get close to. I was a tactile woman, but I found it difficult to touch him. I would give him a kiss but we barely snogged; just a peck here and there on the face, on the cheek.

I looked after him well with home comforts: the wifely chores of cooking, washing, making sure he had fresh sandwiches for work. And I always responded to his sexual advances. Stewart taught me to love better. I mastered a blow job confidently.

Then the bipolar within me took a new turn. I was using excess driven energy in five small part-time jobs. As Stewart paid for the main bills, I only needed to support myself. I left the Scout Association and joined the Guide Association which also led to support worker employment in a primary school. The bipolar was condensed in my head; I knew I mustn't act vocally loud in front of Stewart or I would irritate him. He was a driver; driving is stressful, and he was the type who just wanted a quiet dinner and then to go out pubbing at weekends.

I should have known he wouldn't be a hands-on father like Thomas, but I always try to please the man and I convinced myself he would settle down when he said he wanted children.

I could have requested sterilisation, I was 36, but I kept my options open for him, as he was single and childless.

I seemed to aggravate Stewart a lot.

The attitude from him was put up and shut up. Don't speak when the television is on. Don't discuss anything to do with kids. Don't spend much money. Don't ask for more money. I gave him a daughter quickly into the relationship. Stewart worked away from home so the space created by absent days was a relief. I felt the air was bad around me. I kept hearing voices outside my head telling me different things from different ears, and I was constantly confused. My frustrated voice irritated him. I found it a struggle to cope with raising my daughter on my own. He worked away a lot, and when he was home, he didn't help with caring for our baby girl. He used the excuse that I would have to cope if he wasn't there when working. He didn't see how exhausted I felt, how mentally draining motherhood was. I didn't suffer a mental breakdown after giving birth but physically I was ill a lot and worn out.

I should have realised early into the relationship that the barrier round him would always be raised, and the need for pub life dominated him in his leisure time. I felt driven to break his lifestyle.

Bad decision. I couldn't. We struggled with severe character clashes. I found it hard to accept he wasn't like Thomas who was hands on with children and put his money on the table. I couldn't accept a man spending so much money in a pub. Empty money pissed up the wall. Stewart lost his senses through drink regularly.

When intoxicated he'd twist sentences about and constantly nit-pick. Then, the next day, he would act as if nothing had happened. The way he spoke through drink was hurtful and I felt I was a burden to him even though I nurtured him in a wifely way. I really don't know why we were so confrontational with each other as we still wanted to be together. I felt like there was a huge ill-wind between us, pushing us apart. My empath inner sensitivity found the environment as a common-law wife to Stewart uncomfortable, and his social needs were appalling to me, not pleasing at all, and these made me feel aggravated and ill.

I feel heavy pressure in the air a lot. I absorb the air's sensations. I sense silent invisible things guiding me. Flying around me. Looking after me. Sometimes helping me fight my mind, body and actions, and sometimes working against me, beating me up in my mind. I wake up in the morning and I see angel fairies in the air. They are not people with wings, they are grey and black specks in the air with a figure and an outline of wings. They swoop about all around me in the air. Up and down, around in circles, across the room. They fly about, they don't fall straight to the floor. I feel special. Not everyone wakes up to angel fairies giving a day life pattern. I do. They work their magic fairy dust while swooping around me, and then they go, fade away into the clear air. I don't know why I witness this daily, but I seem to mess up my days more than be productively happy and functional. Therefore, my life has been distorted and I have walked down the wrong alley with conversations, relationships and unpredictable actions. I feel that my head just runs away with itself and I cannot act coherently with sensibility.

I have ESP capability through feelings; I am an empath who absorbs negativity in the environment badly and it crushes me and I make bad decisions daily. The angels gave me the challenge of being Stewart's common-law wife, and I failed that challenge.

I did fail it. I couldn't decipher the way to communicate with him. Poor judgement of my senses. I am not perfect. I was born to face challenges of man and rise again when walking a doomed path.

Sexually Stewart kept me happy; he was hot in his veins and I craved heat from his body. It seemed to warm my veins to be less aggressive. The more he stimulated me between the sheets, the more I felt a euphoric well-being. I was always worn out, so I didn't feel adventurous in my head. I started a family with him, I held down part-time work, so the last thing in my head was entertainment for my partner. Stewart still had a tremendous compulsion to drink at every spare day opportunity. He spent every day off work with his feet under the table in a pub and didn't come back till he was totally off his face in stupefied woozy intoxication. He didn't realise that it incensed me into a mad head of resentful hate. My brain turning black and dense and my mouth volatile in speech. Drunkenness is lowly to me. I see it as a weakness, a person burying their head in a vat of liquor stench. A person losing their senses and becoming a wretched fool. Actions of a man drinking too much alcohol chip my soul. I become bitten and swallowed in despair, anxiety and panic attacks.

I find drunken behaviour immature, ill mannered, selfish, unintelligent and a drunken person twists conversation and talks from their arse.

Stewart and I were chalk and cheese; we had little in common. At the beginning of our relationship he wasn't physically abusive, and I put up with his mental stirrings and suffered in silence. Things changed when his mother died. He became physically aggressive after drink and I never knew what drama would ensue after a night out. Our relationship with each other continued to deteriorate and grew into volatile violent outbursts that neither of us knew how to control.

VIOLENCE

I feel I must describe the violent encounters. People who are subject to domestic abuse are often scared to speak out. I am not. I speak, so others do not feel alone. However, I do realise that men can suffer domestic abuse too, so I can only speak for myself and hope people realise they are not alone when facing an explosive relationship.

A man comes home intoxicated, incoherent, twisting conversation; fear builds in woman. She attempts to diffuse the situation and explains that the situation is different.

Man argues the point, still believing his version is right; man gets physical. Woman's fear seems to breed more physical anger from him. Woman gets pushed. Woman gets slapped. Woman feels broken.

Intoxicated man inherits this crazy head negativity from conversation with others who are not happy, or he cannot cope with the responsibilities in his life. The longer he drinks the more he chats nonsense. He picks up ill thoughts and he vents anger out on his woman.

Woman at home is brunt of the blame. She suffers the pain. He hurls abuse at his woman. She spends too much money. At least she spends it on the kids. He spends his pissing and shitting the shit down the toilet pan. She explains money is for home and clothing, feeding the children. Man gets angry. Woman costs too much. He orders woman to get out of the house with the kids. She does. She is scared.

She walks a mile up the road in snow and ice, barefoot, in her nightie with child in nightie. Man hasn't even let them put on coats and shoes. Thank God there are friends whose home is a sanctuary, and family who let them stay with them. Regular repetitive abuse occurs.

He comes home. Key opens the door. Woman has massive fear of that key opening door. Woman buries head under cover pretending to be asleep. Best plan? Hopeless plan! Man thuds up the stairs, breath thick with liquor poison.

He prods the duvet. *"Wake up. Wake up."*

He stumbles the words out with thick tongue.

He pulls woman's hair on head, he shakes her out of the bed, she falls on the floor.

He shouts that she mis-uses his money.

He shouts that she is a nuisance, a burden.

He stumbles over her drained body crumpled on floor, and lands sprawled across the bed.

This night the woman hasn't even a bed to sleep in. The night is long, when night is disrupted, and woman is distressed.

One sentence out of order, one word out of place, equals one woman falling down the stairs from a push, strangled over a balcony and slapped out of the blue.

The house becomes wrecked. A phone ripped out of a wall. A glass pane cracked in a door. Man doesn't know how it happened the next day. Woman does. She remembers.

She is scared just like the crack across the glass pane. The wounds do not heal easily, and a thin line remains etched in her mind, just like the line in the door.

A child cries hearing night commotion.

"Why is daddy angry? I cannot sleep."

Mum doesn't know how to answer; a part of her wants to protect her child by not damaging daddy's reputation. Children see dad as a hero.

Not an enemy.

Problems are between the adults not the child.

Man devalues the woman who feeds him, makes love to him, breeds his children. How can woman feel worthy? She cannot. How can she love the man and desire him? She feels pained.

The evil force of pain attacks the body tissue. Man cannot stop beating the eyes,

the skin tissue breaks, the pulsating swilling of muscle is compressing the eyes together, the mind condensing into a tight deteriorating state. Woman ripples fearful waves throughout her body.

Man finds it difficult to stop the beating. Man's head is getting carried away. He likes the feel of the pain. Eventually he does stop. Eventually. Selfishness of life in its raw form.

Selfishness, greed and addictive substance need is to blame for man's mixed-up state and violence.

New Year's Eve. My cocktail dress gets burnt in a pub. A woman dancing throws a lit cigarette into my lap. She doesn't like me. He laughs; he says she is jealous of my prettiness. I get upset. I want to go home. I go home.

I tell his niece about the incident; I call him a fool for socialising with imbecile people.

He has walked in the door.

He hears me, he grabs me, he pulls me about, he slaps my face, I fall over, he grabs my legs, he drags me to the front door, he throws me onto an icy January path. I am in my flimsy thin cocktail dress, no shoes, no coat, head smashed against the ice, stunned. He's locked the door. A very happy start to the new year. NOT.

A drunk man doesn't realise the children need a nappy change; the baby needs a feed. Why doesn't he realise that if I am feeding a baby and he gets angry he risks yanking a baby's neck when he pushes me roughly? His niece was my witness to these events, but I wonder how it affected the niece at the time to see domestic violence. She was only a child herself.

I am grateful to his niece for the support she gave. She was there for my children when I needed her. I wasn't there for her though.

Bad of me for letting her witness violence.

Outbursts of a Bipolar Head

How do I explain the outbursts of a bipolar head? The symptoms seem to be one step ahead of my thought processes.

One word from people can trigger terrible consequences of shouting and screaming from me.

One action from people can trigger wild actions physically from me.

Fortunately, I am not naturally aggressive physically. I could be if I was incensed enough, but normally I just do a lot of panicky flapping about, running around headless.

However, if I receive continual lies and deceit or someone tries to mind-control me and confuse me, I can become physically abusive – and man will feel the consequences of his actions.

Bipolar is an action that I have limited control over.

I seem to get irritated by a lot by people's social behaviour.

I have very high standards of how life should be lived.

I have a lot of negative feelings if I think people don't do right for themselves, their family, their children and animals and nature.

I sometimes feel I am sent by God in bodily form to walk on his behalf, so he may witness the destruction that people make to themselves and others.

I am not a Prophet, I don't claim to be anything superior even if it sounds like I do. I just think I am a special energy wave of a person, born into this world to absorb life like a sponge, and react to it verbally when necessary because I cannot stop myself.

Social interaction in society upsets me a lot, and I find it difficult to accept people for who they are. I do find it difficult not to hurt people's feelings; sometimes the venom that comes from my mouth, vocally or by text, is incredibly powerfully rude, insulting, abusive and so hurtful.

I am surprised that people talk to me at all.

Therefore, I walk alone in life; I don't try to form friendships, I stay aloof and people must drift into my circle and fight to keep me as a friend if they are drawn to me.

Therefore, the people I welcome into my life are special and hold a place in my heart permanently.

They are deeply understanding of my inner person, and they accommodate my nature outwardly because they know my heart and soul is pure, giving, generous, humanitarian and loving.

I show my deep inner self in the stories I write which become my printed books. Writing is therapeutic as I can express my anxieties – and other people's anxieties – through the stories I create, and showcase ignorance of issues.

Many authors start the same way before finding the niche that is fruitful for them.

Writing is soul cleansing and fulfilling.

I don't talk to people much in chat, I barely travel anywhere, and I don't socialise much. I never stood in social circles at the school gates, I haven't a girlfriend to go out with regularly socially, and I have always destroyed relationships with men in my life; and men have taken advantage of me, used me and made me unhappy.

I walk away from man eventually.

I realise I hurt his heart and soul and I release his pains and chains to me when the relationship path gets rocky and we cannot walk any further.

Stepping on hot coals for a lifetime in a relationship, burns the sole of your foot to a charcoaled state in the end. Who wants to be a walking cripple if it is a self-infliction or inflicted by a mood-unbalanced person? Best to move on to protect sanity all round. Living life is lonely for a bipolar sufferer.

Bipolar is an illness that means extreme mood fluctuations. Therefore, I firmly stand my ground that we are all walking energy molecules who adapt a body in the timespan we live in, and my energy is wild, and can be uncontrollable even when taking medication.

I found out three years ago I have ADHD within me too.

I have always wondered why I am exceptionally erratic in behaviour even when taking medication.

BRAINWAVES
http://www. brainwavesblog. com

There are 5 brainwaves that ripple through our mind:
BETA, ALPHA, THETA, DELTA, GAMMA.
Mine are incredibly powerful.

BETA is the wave that we use daily in waking life, it's the wave that makes us feel the responses of stress and gives output of a heightened state. People around us, situations around us and the environment will contribute to the actions of BETA. I think my beta airwaves are totally out of control, that's why I am so madcap in daily routines.

ALPHA waves are deep relaxation waves, so people who can meditate, do yoga, or even feel relaxed after drinking alcohol, will heighten this wave. My brain has the least ALPHA and I have always found it incredibly difficult to focus on relaxation. I cannot even sit through a film on television without getting bored or feeling the need to get up. My mind is over stimulated.

THETA is a deep sleep wave, which is activated in a deep sleep; it's when you feel the REM sleep. When you float subconsciously between waking and still sleeping and your eyelids flutter rapidly. It's the type of sleep when you feel as if life is unreal but real. I personally feel things so enhanced in this dream sleep, I often wake up very heavy lidded and unsettled, and in fear of myself, and experience visions and hear things.

This brainwave also encourages my premonitions. I dreamt two large towers breaking up with a plane in them four months before a real tragedy occurred in real life. I remember waking up thinking, who do I tell that this will happen soon? But I realised no one would believe me or prevent it from happening anyway.

DELTA is a deep sleep, where your thoughts detach themselves. This is the space between falling asleep and waking up and not realising you fell asleep. This is the time when your body gets the chance to heal itself a bit, whether you're physically or mentally unwell. I believe this is when God, our supreme energy force, works his magic with the invisible angels and makes the decision to whether we repair and renew ourselves or fall asleep forever. Delta would be nice to lose our life in. Go to sleep and not wake up is the best way to go.

GAMMA is our sensory wave, the wave responsible for filtering information we input into our brains daily. It's the wave that processes the brain's information from all parts of the brain. If you have high amounts of GAMMA it heightens your intelligence, it creates how compassionate you can be, how much self-control you have, and enhances the feelings of well-being and happiness. Learning about this brainwave makes me realise that when I accepted the cognitive therapy to understand my mood swings more, I must have heightened the GAMMA in my head, to become the well-adjusted woman I am today, who blips and bounces back without tipping over to insanity.

I firmly believe in cognitive therapy, 100 per cent. I believe you can change your brain patterns to cope with mental illness better, but it can be a hard fight with your inner self to be fruitful at the end of the insanity tunnel. Hopefully, by understanding brain patterns, everyone who is struggling mentally can help themselves, if they have faith within themselves and belief that they can alter their brainwaves. I constantly pray for everyone in the world to find their own inner peace to live life each day more efficiently.

Sanctuary

I left Stewart to set up home with my three youngsters, a springer spaniel dog and a cat and fish, in an unfurnished rented property in a town. I am a village girl at heart, so it wasn't an easy adjustment.

The feeling was a great relief to be given a key to a new home I could call my own. My close friend Jill put herself out so much to help my great escape, and her family joined in to help me settle in a new home. I am in debt to her and will always value her friendship as a blessing.

My friend Pam also helped me to move on, by taking several bags of clothes and toys and storing them in her own home. *'Mission Haven'* was planned with a precise itinerary. The burdens of my life with Stewart were lifted off my very heavily worn shoulders.

My life was just beginning.

There was a lot to sort out when I first ventured as a single bipolar mother with three children under six years old. Stewart said I would never manage on my own because I was hopeless with money and never had to pay the bills. When you can live life for yourself you either sink or swim. Good job I learned to swim a width; I have got by these last 14 years.

We did eat a lot of take-aways in the first couple of years of being alone. I found it difficult to cope with cooking and cleaning. All my energy was used in ferrying kids to and from school on foot and taking them to after-school activity clubs and making sure they stayed clean and tidy and behaved themselves. So I kept them occupied in after-school activities and played games with them at home.

I found it very difficult to be organised and the house was always messy. I felt as if I was carrying a heavy bag of potatoes on top of my head for the first few single parent years. It was a draining life, to control mood swings and raise children. I constantly felt on trial having to prove I was a decent mother.

Take-aways and Friendships
Balen

I never expected to meet anyone but one evening I ordered a take-away, and a young man delivered me some food. He gave me the once over look with a cheeky glint in his eye and asked if I was single. I said yes, I was, and he said he had a friend working in a local factory who was looking to settle with someone. I was lonely. It was the ninth month of being an isolated single woman and I was missing company. I agreed to give the young man a contact number and I felt quite turned on by the idea of a mystery blind date. I sensed a bipolar buzz of great happiness to meet a stranger, not thinking of any consequences that might go wrong or the danger I was putting myself in with the kids by meeting a stranger.

I have convinced myself all these years that everyone who crosses my path is meant to be. I feel I am protected, and that there is always somebody looking out for me, be it a stranger on the street, my close friends, or people I view in the media. I am convinced that singers, actors and songwriters are special to me, and authors of books, and radio DJs too. All creative people are either angels in human form or heavenly angels watching me invisibly.

A howling wind rattled my window, the candle flickered sending huge flamed shadows across the corner of the wall. I was just settling for sleep and a text message bleeped:

"Can I come and see you" Balen x

I answered back that it was late, and he should contact me the next day. But Balen wanted to see me the same night, he said he worked all day six days a week and he pleaded for me to see him. I gave in.

I opened the door to a small man, small build, dark hair and skin, with a beautiful whitened smile. He was interesting, he was different, he was humble, and his aura glued to mine as soon as he stepped into the house. Balen explained he was looking to settle his life. He said he had political asylum because he had belonged to a nationalist guerrilla group who fought for freedom for their country. I froze. *I had a freedom fighter terrorist stranger in my house.* He seemed so gentle, kind, calm and mild-mannered; it was hard to believe he had held a gun in his hand and shot at planes overhead.

Balen said he was a pacifist, he shot at planes and turned his sight away at the same time. He got shot in the scrotum for his failed bravado. He said he felt strongly it was his duty to defend his country's beliefs, and protect their culture, but for his cowardly actions he had to flee his country. My heart humbled to him, my soul reached out in pity and desire. He was so interesting to know, I accepted him into my home, my heart – and my bed.

Balen was exceptionally loving between the sheets, his soul was so warming, giving, spiritual, and made me feel so loved. The veins of a middle eastern man are so hot, so sexy, and so attentive to a woman's body, I bonded to him straight away. Balen truly worshipped me like a temple.

He told me his father always used to say, that a woman was a man's rock, and if you polish, care, love, and nurture a rock, she would become the most beautiful cut diamond a man could own. Good advice from his father. I was well polished, regularly, daily. Balen was a generous man and he adopted my three children as if they were his own. The only thing that spoilt our relationship was his unsettled status. I couldn't sort his life out, only to give him shelter, food, a ready-made family and womanly comfort.

We had difficulties. I was still very mentally scarred by the life I had with Stewart. I couldn't appreciate Balen's love. He had nicknamed me 'angel' and I should have loved and respected him more. Balen found my bipolar mood swings intolerable. They made his heart hurt. I smashed his phone against a wall, shattered it to smithereens in a jealous rage. His constant phoning to his friends and answering calls made me explosively volatile. I demanded sex so many times to feed the veined aggression; he felt like chopping his organ off and giving it to me. He liked a lot of sex, but I was insatiable. My energy was constantly high, needy, greedy, and ravenous. He was nine years younger than me, and that helped him to cope with me. Balen loved me, but he couldn't handle me. I loved Balen, but I was too lost in my bipolar high swings to realise he was a man, not a robotic phallic stimulator. I gave Balen a key to every hole in my body, as a thank you for his worship and adoration, but I didn't give him the paperwork he needed to sort his life out. Balen found another lady, and secretly dated her. He hadn't the heart to reject me completely. He loved my children as his own and loved me too. He tried to please us both. This failed.

I became obsessively jealous and totally out of control with my actions and ill-thoughts. I sensed he was seeing someone but I couldn't prove it. A take-away delivery driver from the same culture as Balen told me he had seen Balen canoodling a woman at his workplace when he delivered a take-away. The driver felt embarrassed that I looked after Balen with love and care, and accepted his unsettled status and he wanted me to be aware of the cheating. He was so humble and delivered the pizza with his head bowed. I thanked him for his knowledge and told him I had already suspected the two-timing. The delivery man was beaten up by Balen's friends for grassing on a fellow 'brother'. Poor man.

Balen had cheated on me to sort his future life out, and the bipolar in me escalated in full throttle strength.

I flipped and put out 250 posters around my town with his photo, naming and shaming him. I told my youngest daughter I was on a mission when I dropped her off at school, and I defied CCTV systems around the town centre, and people out and about, to put his face on every shop window I could find. I received a letter from a solicitor to tell me to stop exposing him. This incensed me more and I repeated the action again.

This time I put 200 posters in two church graveyards – the same churches I worship in now. This put the clergy in charge in a position to discuss the sanctity of marriage and true love as part of a sermon. Interesting sermon for the congregations. Relationship loss for me.

I moved on alone. Nearly three years of dedicated wasted love. I had pushed another man away from my soul. I asked God if Balen was the one. God answered me no. He wasn't. I had to let him go. I did grieve for him. I grieved for him for over a year.

I became paranoid, obsessive, I even kept a paring knife in my hand bag, determined to not let another woman have him.

I am grateful I didn't tip up enough to use the weapon; my heart didn't mean it really. I had a terrible empty soulless wrench in my gut, of lost love, hope, and emotional security. The bipolar was starved of affection again. I was walking in the wilderness again, my brainwaves starved of heat and love.

My children kept out of my way. When mother is wretched, lost and unloved, its best to just hide in the bedroom and hope she gets over it.

My poor kids suffered through my inability to hold down a relationship.

I apologise for the emotional hurt and stress I caused them, when they were all too young to understand. At least I had my kids. My children are still there, when man fails to make me happy.

Murat

When I feel a man is special to me, I feel an aura or a yearning. I first set eyes on Murat in my local newspaper. I was still in an unhappy relationship, full of turmoil, with Stewart. I scanned my local paper and always enjoyed viewing the wedding day pages. A handsome man and cute woman were posing for a photo and I immediately noticed his foreign-sounding name, and his incredible likeness to my first love Thomas. He was like the foreign version of Thomas.

The young lady was pretty and cheerful looking, but I noticed they were standing apart in the photo, not close together, nor in an embrace or loving look. I really fancied the guy and wished it was me having another chance at young love and marriage. I had already started a second family with Stewart, having three young children between his drinking binging bouts. I left the image of the supposedly happy couple, with their odd stance, closed the newspaper and silently wished them both a happy life. I carried on with my tormented present one.

Ten years later, single parent life was hard to juggle. It's very easy for people to say that being a single parent affects an abundance of families, but to juggle kids, home life and insane head thoughts with crazy mood swings that couldn't be tapered down by the psychiatric profession was horrendous. I found it difficult to apply myself to simple jobs like cooking a decent meal in safety. All the medication to date sedated me heavily and it piled on weight or gave me dreadful side effects.

I finished with Balen and felt isolated at home again, lacking in emotional security. I also felt a loss in my soul and yearned for the space to be filled again of loving in abundance. I started to order take-away food again; my cooker was ailing, and my spirit hoped I'd find another hot-blooded foreign man.

I befriended a voice over the phone – a man always answered my take-away request. He spoke English clearly, and had a lovely accent when he spoke. My ears trembled at the sound of him and my heart waves fluttered to match the ear trembles.

This man was special, I felt him through the phone. I felt his aura through my ears. I wanted him.

We chatted every time in between ordering the food and I pieced his life together by brief phone chat. He seemed so unhappy and he enjoyed brief flirtatious chats in my voice. I had found out by the delivery drivers that he was married but unhappy.

He had settled his life hastily to secure his future.

I am not the type of person to come between couples struggling to keep a marital relationship, so I stood back for a year and just listened to his woes over the phone. The take-away shop staff were very happy to take my order and I rang them three or four times a week requesting a delivery just to hear his voice. I never met him during this time – he was stuck in a kitchen cooking. He was married with problems. He was out of bounds. I didn't know what he looked like either.

One year on I received a phone-call from a private number. Murat, the sexy-voiced take-away man, had rung me to say he had left his wife and job and was living and working elsewhere. I was pleased he had told me that he had moved on, and I was still on my own, so I offered him coffee and chats if he needed company. He thanked me for my kindness, and said he'd think about it. I heard nothing more for another few months.

I was still lonely at Christmas as the children went to stay with their father. Christmas Eve is spiritual for me, because it's an important event for Polish people to celebrate, the star shining for Jesus's birth, and I didn't want to spend it alone. I felt low and lonely and it spurred on an erratic bipolar 'need'. I rang the take-away shop and when they answered; *"What would you like to order?"* I said, *'A man!'*.

The person handling the call laughed and stated that there

weren't many men in the shop at this festive time, but they did have one in the kitchen they could deliver, if he came with a food order. I wasn't hungry for food, I was hungry for loving; I wanted my veins to pulsate sexiness and heat. I needed to expel a lot of excess built up manic energy.

I ordered food to keep the shop happy.

Murat was pushed into my house with a good luck sign from his driver. He stood in front of me, head stooped and cowering. He was tall, handsome, and my foreign Thomas. I knew it was my telephone man from his first greeting of "Hi, be kind to me". I felt sad he feared me, but happy that I finally met the sexy toned voice.

Murat was the groom in the wedding photo. He was meant to be in my life. God brought him to me.

Murat spent the night with me. He told me his tale of jumping overboard from a merchant navy ship, with a friend, and swimming two miles to the English shore to seek a better life. He unfortunately entered a bad life with little respect from the lady he married.

He bred three kids with her, and she mentally abused him a lot. She didn't care for him in loving and home comforts and told him to live off pizzas in his work place. She constantly got drunk, and taunted him, by giving him a gimmicky dancing flower singing

"Row, Row, Row your boat".

He was mentally beaten up, his head was constantly in a frozen vacant state, and I made it my task to etch away each furrowed line in his forehead with massaging love.

I fell for him deeply; my soul wanted him. He was tremendously hard work to love, and to keep satisfied. His organ was massive and I realised what was meant by the phrase 'to be hung like a donkey'. I used a lot of bipolar sexual steam on Murat. We kept each-other happy. He was living apart from his family in his own flat, but he had got into debt and wanted to move in with me for a while.

He did, and we had a very warm close friendship, but his emotional barrier was huge. This was the first time I had witnessed a beaten-up man.

I was always obsessed by my own problems and by my own mental scarring I didn't realise that even men suffered at the hands of their spouse or partner. We had a lot in common, we became very close friends. We were both worn out battered minds trying to survive.

My mental health stabilised at this point. Murat worked afternoons till late at night, so we had some wonderful cosy times while the kids were at school. He was strong as a lover and fulfilled my high energy needs fabulously. I was brimming with well-being and passion and much needed heat. The relationship with Murat was special. He divorced his wife because he sensed that the third child was not his. He had a DNA test, and this proved he had provided for a child who had been fathered by another man.

I was the first one to know the DNA result. I felt special that he wanted me to be the first to know. Murat told me that he never felt heat from his third child, he knew he hadn't fathered the child. Murat describing 'heat' echoes my belief about feeling auras.

Passionate Murat could feel the auras of his children.

Auras are energy waves. Auras are vibes, but not many people know how to tune into these airwaves.

Murat only lived with me for a short while, but we had a very loving time and he still means a lot to me in my heart.

When he left my life, he kissed me on my breast and said thank you to me for being in his life.

Such a romantic gesture to kiss the mammary of a mother. This gesture from him showed me respect and gratefulness.

"A man who takes me into his arms, holds my heart forever. My soul spreads into tiny pieces and a piece stays in the soul of a man who's loved me with his heart. A twinkle from my eye lightens up my piece of soul in his heart and warms him a loving temporary glow, and if we meet by accident, a man feels his heart glowing again."

Something good comes out of a whirlwind like me.

I am a loving woman, when man loves me, and I spoil him by nurturing and caring domestically.

Frogs, Toads, and Flirt Loads

Bipolar is a flirtatious illness, If one is hyper or manic, one feels such a huge sense of natural well-being. This is truly a gift to have, as you don't need the highs of drink, cigs or drugs. Countless men crossed my path in a flirtatious way with no sexual connection. I give out huge vibes when sexually high but exercise control. Thankfully.

Ranvir a cheeky young man who served me bread and pop, but who claimed to have an erect manhood as soon as I entered his shop. A bit young to enter me. A tadpole not a frog!

Adam a plumber who fixed a shower on taps on his knees but wanted me instead of a cup of tea.

A toad, he had a family!

David who delivered the local city papers for me to sell, wanted a quick kiss and no tell.

A toad, he had a family!

Bruce built like a tank and pursued me for years, a jack the lad who would have left me in tears.

A big bullfrog!

Chris a policeman who patrolled our street, he hoped I'd give him a mouth swallowed treat. No trust for me, not going there. A toad.

Ricki who met me on a street, begged me for attention to perk up his meat. Too young. A Tadpole.

Ali 1, Ali 2, Ali 3 and 4, loads of Alis, no orgies amour. Army of frogs.

Pete who worked in a bar fancied me, but being a bi, didn't do anything for me. I don't mean bipolar either! A frog.

Sara and hubby from on line, both wanted me for a jolly good time. They pursued me for three years in chat. TOADS.

Mohammed was rich or, so he said, offered me laptops and jewellery if he could get into my bed. Difficult, he was in Saudi. Nice frog.

Nick the Greek, worth a bob or two, wanted me as a gambling dolly, on his arm as a charm. Free holidays, house makeover.

I'm the toad! I should have accepted loads!

Abundance of men asked for 'a three' sadly to all I said it's *NOT* me. Frogs, toads, tadpoles.

Just a selection of worshippers that my eyes have drawn in. My loyalty is to God, not the male species evolved from sin.

I truly don't think I could love a man whole heartedly. I am a million miles away from human man in my heart; my spirit can be receptive, and it's nice to be wanted, and occasionally someone gets lucky, for a while.

Writing in a poetic rhyme is another sign of fluctuating high moods. I get these often.

I cannot help being sexual and I don't mean to lead men on. I exude a buzz of sexual mania and I start expressing myself visually to all. I flirt sexually, I talk sexually, I breathe sexually, my mannerisms can seem enticing, but I equally change moods and I can be frightening.

Special people look beyond my many changing faces. They are the people who stay in my life. Others I let go. I always move forward, never backwards. My path is marked, and I am guided. I do have choice.

I am lucky that I never found myself in an awkward moment with a man, who could have been potentially dangerous for me. I still feel I am a protected 'species'; I have felt this all my life. I strongly believe that the foreign lovers were supposed to be in my life. I believe that in their 'past' lives they were nomads who followed the star that shone for Jesus's birth. They now flocked around me to protect me. Their blood was special – I felt it deeply. Balen told me that in a bipolar ranting moment I said that my mother felt close to his birth land. I put my two knuckles on my hands close together on a map.

Who knows where my mother's soul was in a previous life? In the past, Earth's land was a super continent called Pangaea. Maybe my mum's energy wave 'gene' background was closer to Balen's homeland than we know.

Why would I say these things? I must feel them. Surely?

Aram

Aram was very young when I popped in the town shop for a bite to eat. He watched me through the CCTV camera as he prepared my order and, as I paid for it, I noticed a scribble under the flap of wrapped-up paper. He had written his mobile number. I smiled at the mobile number but declined to log it or get in touch.

I like having a younger lover, but not *that* young.

Over a period of eight weeks, Aram sweet-talked me at every opportunity when I went into the shop or ordered some food from home. Eventually he infiltrated my phone number from his shop's records – which I admired as he could have lost his job – and begged me through text to be my man.

I moved on from Murat and had no one else. I gave in to Aram, whose soul was pure, and I felt a deep aura of holy values in his blood. I doubted he'd keep me happy in bed, but I was wrong. He was heavenly, and I felt a strong magnetic glowing bond developing between us. He was a true gift from God. Pure, honourable, loving and promised to his first cousin back in his homeland.

I felt honoured that he chose me to be in his life.

He had eight years to wait for his cousin to be his wife – that's some wait when you cannot even be intimate with her on returning home. Aram said to me that,

"a woman is worth waiting for if a man's heart burns with her truth and love".

You cannot beat a middle eastern man for romantic words. HEAVENLY. I wished I was her.

Aram stayed in my life for two years. Pure gold that young man. He calmed my bipolar the best. Very apt his name, which means Calm. I will never forget him.

Abdul

The time with take-away men ran its course; my bipolar was erratic and the foreign men helped to stabilise the moods, and I decided to spend more time chatting with people on dating sites. Online chat became my world in-between relationships. The internet is like one big coffee morning of chat if you are trapped in your home with children to care for. Abdul came into my life through a chat with a man online who said he knew someone who was 'different'. My head buzzed hyper again with interest.

The man said he'd tell his friend to speak to me online. My heart skipped a beat. A glow rippled the veins.

"Hi. I am Abdul" a handsome young man made himself known to me on a dating site. *"I would like to get to know you."*

He seemed sincere, in the text message.

I looked at his appearance and I wasn't drawn to his photo, but his culture was interesting, and he seemed to look innocent outwardly.

I have a very deep dense heavy feeling in the pit of my stomach behind my belly button. I firmly believe that this is a gut guidance I must follow.

My path is written but I do have a choice whether to listen to my gut or not.

My emotions are magnified far more than those of other people.

The gut reaction creases my stomach to act on a situation; it makes me double up and feel sick.

My gut was beckoning this special man.

I became defensive at first, saying he was too young, too far, and I couldn't support his cause.

He was disappointed and said if I changed my mind, he would welcome it. I left it there but couldn't forget him. I used to chat to lots of people in a day, 20 at a minimum and 50 maximum, so what made Abdul different?

The feeling in gut is a dragging stomach urge.

The stomach is pulling me to go back to the situation.

I tried to forget him over five days, and he never tried to get in touch after that one conversation.

I texted him through the dating site. I told him I lived near the train station, and welcomed him for a weekend visit, even though I didn't feel outwardly drawn to him through his photo.

I welcomed him into my home as a stranger.

Abdul walked up the garden path.

"He's here kids," I shouted.

I looked out of the window. Abdul looked different as a man. He was far better looking in real life.

I opened the door and he nervously kissed me on the cheek as he entered. I could see his shyness; I felt his purity.

This man was a virgin. He didn't need to tell me – I sensed it; I felt his aura. No wonder the friend on line said he was different.

I made a huge spread of ethnic food that would appeal to him. I am very accommodating with man's home 'comforts' so I adapted myself to his food requirements.

I am a formidable, opinionated woman, but my soul is subservient to looking after man.

Abdul was overwhelmed with my kindness and hospitality. He liked my children, he felt welcome.

Something stirred between the two of us; we both flushed heat in table chat over food. Our eyes bonded in a sexual magnetism that I had never felt before.

I felt as if something else was drawing us together.

We both felt panic attacks at the same time, we both coughed at the same time, we both felt a passionate urge at the same time. This was all just sprung on us both without a flirtatious conversation.

When the kids went to bed, we found it hard to chat with comfort. We were fighting sexual feelings with a raised barrier.

Abdul requested to go outside to light up a cigarette.

I felt humbled by his politeness. He looked at me through the window and waved to me to come outside.

I went outside and he grabbed me for a passionate kiss. I was surprised and the kiss was clumsy, an on the spur naïve moment.

"I would like to stay with you, I need to develop my English language. I miss family life. I want a woman's love."

He took me by surprise. I never expected this conversation, from a first meeting.

"Would you commit to my faith and beliefs?" he asked.

Good job I was a free spirit and welcomed all cultures into my spiritual soul. The young guy wasn't asking for much. My soul screamed out it was meant to be. I was on another challenging path to explore man.

I studied religions and faiths of the world, so I ventured into his faith with honesty, loyalty and commitment within my heart. I became his wife on the day before my birthday, and I had lots of things to learn to please him.

I was willing to become his wife because I felt love for him from my soul.

Marriage in the Qur'an:

(SWT means)

"Subhanahu wa ta'ala"

"May He be glorified and exalted."

Allah SWT says in the Qur'an:

"And among His Signs is this, that He created for you mates from among yourselves that ye may dwell in tranquillity with them, and He has put love and mercy between your (hearts): verily in that are Signs for those who reflect"

(Qur'an 30:21)

Alhamdulillah
All praise is for Allah

Respecting and understanding a partner's belief and cultural upbringing is the foundation of a mutual loving relationship. Ignorance is rife in society. Sadly.

Commitment

When I enter a relationship, I enter one hundred per cent from my heart. I actively learn everything to make my man comfortable: his eating patterns, his desires, his beliefs – and I see this as my respect for him. Abdul taught me the way to pray by an iPhone digital diagram. The way forward is through technology, it seems.

This took the shine off wholesome spirituality.

Abdul's mother taught me to cook via his laptop; she didn't speak English, so it was a good job that cooking only needs looking. My children seemed to like Abdul – he was young and very energetic and made time for them. Sexually I was satisfied but unfortunately bipolar twists and turns its own way, so no matter what the environment is, the mood changes do their own thing.

Abdul found it difficult to cope with my fluctuations. He spent more time in the bedroom than in the communal living room, to escape my shouts.

He videoed me once on his phone to show my psychiatric community nurse how crazily I spoke randomly in chat.

I seem to drone when bipolar goes too high and my voice is gibberish and I don't stop to breathe in between.

I flay my arms about a lot too and drop things on the floor, and rant abusive language repetitively loudly.

On the one hand, a man in a relationship with me finds me hard work, on the other, he finds me exciting in mannerism and speech.

The energy I exude in sexual play drives man full on with sexual desire but then equally I can become withdrawn and uncommunicative when troubled over something.

My brain seems to switch on and off in all directions randomly. I am quite girlish in bed, I tease with my eyes, and tease him with my fingers. Massages, food games and constant tactile touch. My anger seems to turn a man on, but my erratic body signs off. I am so sharp in jerking movements – I can appear to be scary. I don't actively intend to swop partners I just feel a man getting head worn with me and I care enough to let him go.

Abdul and I exchanged marital vows in a beautiful informal ceremony with six religious men present.

I felt so special, and the whole ceremony was conducted in Arabic and repeated to me in English.

At the end of the ceremony sweets were exchanged and I was presented with some flowers.

I felt fulfilled spiritually but unfortunately did not gain my elderly aunt's blessing.

She was the only surviving relative to show her disapproval but I went ahead anyway as I am a stubborn woman when I want to do things my way.

Abdul had the blessing of his mum and five brothers and sisters, but not from his father.

Abdul spoke to his father via internet chat.

His father requested to see me on web cam.

Arabic conversation was exchanged, and Abdul's face changed. He shut down his laptop, his face dropped.

I asked him what his father said.

He told me his father thought I was pretty for a mature woman, and young looking, but I wouldn't bear him a grandchild. He told Abdul to take me over to their country; he would dress me in a burka, and accept me as his second wife and stare at my beautiful eyes forever more.

I was shocked. I asked Abdul what his mother would have thought to that idea.

Abdul said his mother looked old and felt worn; she had six children and she would have gladly accepted me to please her husband and to have help with the cooking for the family.

I made a mental note not to board a plane to visit Abdul's family. Such a shame, his brother and sisters liked me and so did the mum, but his father was a bit greedy to want another wife, and he wasn't going to have me. I didn't like bushy thick beards anyway. I was beard-phobic. I realised that Abdul's future was in disarray, our time together was limited and, from then on, I suspected Abdul was planning a great escape.

Abdul wasn't happy. He had come to England for a temporary educational visit, and although he had acquired jobs in a bar and a restaurant, he didn't earn much money. His original intentions were honourable. He wanted the love and comfort of a mature woman and family life, and he wanted me to have support, love and a chance to move forward with my life.

Good intentions, but bad luck circumstances. I knew something was going wrong when he invited his best friend to stay for a weekend.

Abdul's friend didn't want to mix with my children. He hid his face, pretending that he was shy. He and Abdul were having secret Arabic chats, but I could tell by their body language that they were planning something. My body started to put out very negative vibes. I felt a dense and heavy feeling in the pit of my stomach. Outwardly I shook, and wind waves created around me.

Abdul and his friend went out to meet friends in another city. After they had gone, while I bustled busy with the housework, I felt the air vibes whipping up around me, my mind became full of turmoil, anxiety and panic attacks.

I rang Abdul. I was gibberish, I shouted down the phone that he was leaving me. He told me to calm down – he was job hunting with his friend and trying to find a bedsit for his friend. I didn't believe him. I slammed the phone and cut off his conversation. He tried to ring me several times but I didn't answer. Airwaves around me pushed me into a hurried frenzy running state.

I gathered his personal documentation, his laptop, notebook and clothes. I asked a neighbour to look after them. I rang Abdul again and told him I was going to hand in all his belongings to the police. They could deal with him. I told him to not come home. He was deceitful and had used me as a stepping stone. I scared him so he returned from the city to calm me down and left the train station to walk to my home.

He turned on his heels and fled back to the city after hearing my wild angry threats.

The strength of airwaves in my home was so powerful and I had pushed him away with a mighty force.

God had told me he was the wrong man too.

God was right. Abdul arrived at my home as a pure untouched spiritual man, but his spirit got tarnished while living with me.

He witnessed the permissiveness of young people in town and it made him lust for things which his faith didn't approve of. He had viewed things on line behind my back at a time when he taught me to be holy for a month.

He had even advertised to meet young girls in our town. The devil had gripped him, and I received the vibes to let him go. I pushed him away with relief.

He divorced our spiritual matrimonial relationship by phone call, with my psychiatric community nurse as a witness to our conversation. He said he couldn't fault me as a wife, or a lover. I taught him to fly in bed, and he was grateful for the extra English language, literacy and reading support. He said he couldn't trust me, he needed to move on and stabilise his life elsewhere.

God pushed Abdul out of my life. Yet another man failure. I listen to God not man. I moved on.

The experience of being in his life was worth it.

I have no regrets. The relationship was meant to be. Poor bipolar crazed me.

Nine signs of a man moving on

1. When he hides information he is viewing and smiles creepily.
2. When he buys suitcases unexpectedly.
3. When he sorts out all his clothes and folds them neatly stacked.
4. When he makes a lot of phone calls in succession, planning jobs, rooms, and escape routes.
5. When he never goes to bed and stays up all night, trying to avoid intimacy.
6. When he hides letters he receives, or documents he gained.
7. When he goes to visit friends at every opportunity.
8. When he ignores the children and stops giving them his time.
9. When he stops thanking you for kindness and home comfort and you know he wants to be elsewhere.

I started to meet English men after the foreign men. I hoped I would find a more stable life, but all I found were men with drinking issues. My fault. I chose to socialise in a pub but soon realised the life was boring, the people were two-faced and fake in their relationships, and to witness drunkenness is appalling; people have no integrity and show no decorum.

Bible verse:

"Nor thieves, nor the greedy, nor drunkards, nor reviler, nor swindlers will inherit the kingdom of God."

1 Corinthians 6 :10

I gave two men the chance to be in my life – Alan and Peter. I am a good woman and I can be exciting, loving and nurturing. I dated both for two years at different times but gained no joy with either of them. The drink was under their skin, and woman cannot fix a man who has lifelong habits.

I tend to see these people as free-spirited, unwilling to settle down with one woman, and who like chasing women. They get bored easily. I fell for Peter with my heart and soul. He was attractive in maturity and we had bipolar in common; we also enjoyed writing and literature. I wanted him to be stable in a new life. Unfortunately, when people socialise in pubs for many years, they tend to make friends with a few women, and I have a terrible jealous possessive nature, so this didn't bode well with my trust issues, and I couldn't accept Peter having single women friendships. He wouldn't have liked it if I had had single men as friends.

Life with Peter was fun when he wanted me to himself and annoying when he showed his personality issues.

He was constantly in denial of his illness and the personalities he portrayed. Our friendship was spoilt by people who were jealous of our close bonding and companionship, they interfered and encouraged him to go to social events, which contributed to his excessive drinking. I loved Peter, but he didn't know how to love me back; he based love on stimulation. He wanted to be needed and drink happily with someone. I am too head-strong to need anyone, and I don't need drink in my life. I found him hard work to love because he didn't believe the love, I felt for him.

Neither of my daughters thought a man of Peter's age was suitable for me because I get overpowering and demanding and possessive.

However, Peter brought the best out of my creative mind and he was meant to be the stepping stone for my writing enthusiasm.

My sexual energy is explosive when stimulated, so an older man of Peter's age would find me too much to cope with. I used to scare younger men away.

I have a volatility in my genes that spreads in all manner

I always say that people and animals cross my path for a reason, and that reason links up to the next bit of my journey, to move forward in time.

I am waiting to know where my path leads to, be it through animal or human, and although I remain single with no one since Peter, you never know who can cross my path to gain my attention and love.

Overleaf I have written a poem called 'Shamed'.

It shows the hurt and deceit I feel when man doesn't admit to being disloyal.

Lies and twisting tales do not settle well with me; my head becomes angry and I blow up like a volcano.

Kate Dobrowolska

Shamed

Do you know how much my soul wanted you?
it preyed in my belly the fulfilment need,
the feelings like ripples of starved despair,
knowing that you wandered out there.
You like all women they please your eye,
my heart hurts and my soul cries.
I feel hollow because it is wrong,
the women you know are darkened souls.
I am light within, I am woman with spirit of man.
The difference between them and I you see,
they seek, greed, money, support and need!
and all I desire is a heart who **loves** *me.*
I am a pure soul from the Earth's core,
and I aim to stand proud and serve our lord,
there's no way I will die without return,
I have heaven's key, here on Earth's floor.
I was born to witness man,
and destruction of life,
the way he behaves and treats a wife.
I can never be yours anymore,
your hands are tarnished with past at your door,
Your inner soul says what you must do, and
shows you are dark, bitter, a liar, and untrue.
If you stay with the light and lighten your life.
without the drinking liquor, to help you get by,
you will have hope to be soulfully happy,
and receive another chance,
to improve your mind rhythm,
and enjoy living a surreal dance.

Family and Woman Thoughts

I have never been drawn to women as friends, but I have allowed some to get to know me during my adult life and I believe they are very special women.

I truly believe that in spirit they have been part of my past. I feel warmth when I accept people into my heart – the emotional attachment is strong.

I have also been blessed with two daughters, and although we have character clashes, I am glad that both of my girls have different personalities to myself and to each other, as to have two clones of my character would have been tragic, as both girls and I have strong characters.

We are warrior women, but we manage to avoid too many explosions between ourselves.

I also have three sons, who all have a very strong personality in different ways, so genetically there is something about me that strength is prominent in 'will' and I have passed this on to the children.

I don't socialise with people much because I feel different, and even in working life I have always preferred to be in charge, or work alone, or work in a man's environment. I walk in wilderness alone.

Relationships

I never go back to a relationship because you cannot fix a relationship when the parts are worn and broken, as the same problems will occur. I see it as man's loss; they probably see it as my loss. I am maturing on the wrong side of 50 but I know if I really wanted a man for company, I could easily get one.

I am happy with my writing, dog, and not mixing with people, to avoid confrontations and hurt. My heart has given up on finding love, but who knows if my soul will find another soul? Our souls are independent within our body in life, and after death, and I might accept someone else into my life if my soul gets drawn to someone.

Friends. We All Need Them

I have three close friends who have remained solid and supportive throughout my life: Joyce, Pam and Jill. I asked each of them to write a description about my bipolar symptoms and my personality. My friends don't know each other personally or socialise with each other. They all live in different areas.

Joyce has known me since birth. We lived opposite each other on the same street and our mothers were friends. Joyce moved away at eight years old but our 'sisterly' love for each other is strong and we have kept the friendship from afar. We see each other once or twice a year. We have bonded childhood souls.

Pam has known me since infant school and she grew up near me on the next street. Pam and I went through school life together and we shared our childhood, our school life and our adult life till this day, although we don't see each other much in present times. We remain strong bonded childhood souls.

Jill I met as a young adult in the late 1980s. She was a rep for Tupperware, and I was an Avon rep, but we became firmer friends when her daughter joined my Rainbow Guide group in 1996, and our friendship has grown closer in 23 years. Jill is a wonderful soul. I am sure she has telepathic instincts as she always seems to know when I need her company or lacking in something. Instinctively, she visits and brings me things that I am short of. A very special lady and I feel she knows me from a past life somehow.

My Friends' Character Statements about Bipolar Me (How I appear to others in mood swing)

Joyce's Observation

Joyce says that when I am calm, I think more slowly, my speech tone is lower, and I speak without judgement of others. When I become bipolar high, she doesn't know who I am as a person. I change. I cannot relax. I find it difficult to multi-task, I constantly look worried, I am loud in speech and I try to get my words out in a rush. I am erratic in speech. Joyce says I stutter as I speak and I become more opinionated and judgemental of others, when it's sometimes best to say nothing at all. I paint a spade a spade and my honesty can be hurtful to others.

Joyce sees beyond my troubled mind and says I have a big heart; I would help anyone and be generous if I could afford to. My strengths are: I pick myself up and brush myself down. I am strong for my children and selfless. I am clever when stable, and she feels I have been dealt a bad card with the bipolar leading me down wrong paths. My weaknesses are that I don't think before I speak, and I fall into relationships too quickly and have bred too many children, when I struggle to control my own health.

She says that I don't take a breath in conversation when high, neither do I listen to others. She feels she understands my moods better now, but believes I get carried away with relationships and that I get involved with people I barely know because I bond to them too quickly.

Joyce has been hurt by my bipolar outbursts but because she lived away from me, she couldn't understand why I hurt her heart at the time. Our friendship has developed over the years and she realises that I am plagued with this bipolar mind.

She says I am a lovely person.
She must think this way. She has stayed in my life.
Thank you mate. X

Pam's Observation

Pam feels I try harder with my appearance when I feel better about myself. I am very expressive with my hands and body language when high. I become fidgety and restless when feeling down. When we meet, I manage to have a smile and a laugh with her, but Pam can never be sure which emotion she's going to be greeted by when we meet. I am preoccupied with my own problems when feeling negative and can be critical of other people when suffering mood swings.

I say what I feel is right or wrong. I don't take in other people's opinions. Nothing holds my attention for long, including the numerous employment oportunities I have had. I am impulsive, but I make the best out of the situation I put myself in. I do try to make my relationships work.

I have lifted Pam's spirit at times, by producing friendship cards and sending endearing small tokens out of the blue. Pam feels I try to please others most of my life.

I married on impulse to get away from home.

I am generous and warm natured, when I have time to give to someone. Pam feels I have always been a good mate, and she feels we have always been there for one another, spiritually too. She says I have done the best for my kids and she knows they appreciate me, even if I think they don't at times.

I must go forward one day at a time and worry about the future as it happens. We are all imperfect, I'm not alone.

Sound advice from a sound great mate. Thank you. X

Jill's Observation

Jill said she can tell by the type of text I write whether I am high or low. I am a very impulsive person who sometimes doesn't think things through before I write or speak, when high.

I also won't listen to reason when I am low.

If my mind is calm with a level head, I am prepared to listen more slowly to reason.

If my mind is higher and erratic, I talk faster, irrationally and in a high-pitched voice. My emotions can hurt at times, but I realise my mistake and try to rectify the situation. My life pattern has concerned Jill over the years; she didn't agree with the friendships I formed, but she knows I am stubborn and go ahead with my plans anyway.

In Kate's words: *"It's my illness, my needs."*

As a friend Jill has always been there to support me and help me but feels she doesn't want to criticise me, as my family haven't really understood my illness, so she feels she is my shoulder to lean on.

Jill feels I am vulnerable when suffering bipolar swings.

My character is strong, and I can be very positive, and sometimes I am over generous, and people take advantage of me. My weakness is I am impulsive and over-react too quickly. Overall, I am caring with a heart of gold and it's not my fault I have a condition that unbalances my state of mind.

She feels I was born into a harsh life where things were kept in the dark. There is more constructive support in the society we live in now and if I had been born now, I would have had a better network of care.

Thank you Jill my mate. X

The three ladies hesitated in producing their statements. All three ladies joked that our friendship may diminish by truthful facts.

Never, ladies. My human angels were formed the day I was born, and you all have been my anchors when I have not been able to cope. I love you all.

My friends were chosen for me.

Deep Thoughts

My girlfriends are my human angels gifted to me to help me ride the mood waves of discontent. We adapt human bodies to keep the world growing and evolving. I believe in the karma and in reincarnation. I believe there is a connection to all life forms, which evolve in a never-ending circle which never repeats itself. You do not get the chance to live the same body life a second time, that's why people try to live life to the full. However, I do know that some people can temporarily reincarnate and become a fresher faced similar person but whether they stay in the body form permanently I do not know; they might just have a temporary mission. I met two people on the street of my town at separate times of life, but the eerie thing is I knew they were dead; they had returned to show me to keep believing in the afterlife which I do. I also feel that St Michael the archangel warrior defender is in my area watching over me. I cross his path many times and he's given me a stare into my eyes and a knowing look, yet he is real but a stranger.

I do believe the obscene cruel species of man and beast will perish into the Earth's natural resources and I know that there are more good humans than bad ones on this Earth now, and this will stay for as long as the Earth isn't destroyed by man's greed and bad decisions of power and influence.

A supreme energy entity powers life with the sun, moon, stars and planets, with sea and light, giving us our natural sources for growth and productivity.

We are now governed by the cosmos, because the spiritually good have overcome the bad in numbers.

The energy waves in air draw in humans to complete a destiny life cycle as planned but can change course by our own bad mind decisions. We all have an invisible energy barrier. We are mapped out from birth according to the line-up of the planets and sun and stars and our region of birth. We are just a link in a long never-ending chain, and this continues until death and our particles reform elsewhere. Just one piece of dead skin cell can regrow something if it latches on to the right environment to develop. Upon death our last breath expels and surges on as an energy wave waiting to rest into something. It's quite unsettling to know but we could naturally clone ourselves within other people by our energy wave. I know this in mind thought but I have a human body at present, so I really don't know how that happens. On a few occasions I have seen a picture or met a person and feel close to them as a stranger, as if they were a part of me or a part of someone in my family.

Doctors who perform transplants of human organs are wonderful skilled people because they allow the living to carry on living but also allow the deceased to be part of someone else too. I haven't needed a transplant of an organ, but it would be interesting to talk to someone who has some one-else's organ. I just haven't met anyone who has this life saving blessing to ask them if they feel they are a part of someone else. I say what my gut feels is right or wrong. I am impulsive, but I make the best out of the situation I put myself in. I do try to make my relationships work, but I feel that airwaves around me contribute to pressurising me and suffocating me causing aggressiveness to develop. Negativity has a lot to answer for too; it causes problems to fester badly in mental and physical illness, and accounts for freaky environmental weather conditions and injuries from unexpected events.

Brothers, Sons, and Daughters

I feel a very strong emotional bonding towards males in my family line. I sometimes feel my own chemical make-up is manly within. The sense of genetic connection to my brothers has been very strong from my birth. They have extended families now and are grandparents, and I don't see them as much as I would like to, but in messaging and visiting I feel the warmth is still there, and they both look out for me in their own way.

My sons are a mixed bag of personalities, but I feel their pains more strongly than I feel my daughters.

I love my daughters, but I have a sense of detachment with both. I think there's an invisible gap between the girls and myself, and I am grateful for that because if they were born into a similar look, personality and emotions, I think we could have been a volatile family. That's why some families lose a grip with their own family lines because they are evolved genetically 'cloned' and inherit 'clone personalities' and if a family has angry personalities and moods it could be a time bomb problem for arguments brewing and festering.

Soul

Souls are invisible energy and only highly perceptive people can recognise these in the air and environment outside another person's vision.

An interesting scenario cropped up recently. I spotted two baby crows in my garden that had been pushed out of their nest too early; they were cute to watch in character and habits. Sadly, one of them died in a tangle of thorns. This crow had tried to hide in a tangled thorny bush when his sibling refused to share the habitat and bullied him.

This was very upsetting for my daughter and myself, but the same evening as I was writing, a shadowy black winged blur came across my head, and therefore this is the reason I feel strongly about souls as energy and realms of dimensions that move them.

Our particles of matter move on and reform as something new. We come from death, so we must grow into life, or perish within structures. Karma is real and you are what you are, and you evolve into another inherited form of life; you never come back as the same; the evolution moves on in a different manner, a different time span, something different, but something that can equally fall bad on you. So stay positive to have a positive everlasting journey…

Never underestimate love, because love can break boundaries beyond our dreams and improve and alter our destiny. If you live a life of evolving love, kindness, peace, adventure, humility, compassion, faith and care, you cannot walk a wrong path after spreading that in your lifetime. Ironically, I am a mixed up, emotionally distorted human being, who appears unkind outwardly. I know the kindness I show, and I feel the past I have lived through formerly was far worse than the past

I have lived through in this life – but I don't remember my last life other than I have felt my mother's Second World War years deeply.

Hopefully my next one will be a bird or a butterfly, so I can fly again in a more peaceful manner.

This life has been the most challenging journey I have taken, because I was born to absorb everyone's energies; my mind and body has been suffocated a lot. Atlas was punished by Zeus in Greek mythology and was made to hold up the heavens on his shoulders, which I imagine made him hunched back! I feel I am holding this Earth together by the root of the sole of my feet.

I have always suffered terrible circulation issues in my legs, and experienced a rising thrombosis a few years ago. Aspirin and raising legs help and if thrombosis starts in the leg and doesn't reach higher than the knee, you can heal yourself. I am walking more heavily and stiffly now as if the atmosphere and changes in the universe are bearing down on me from my child-bearing hips downwards; I feel lightheaded and dizzy a lot too. However, I know that many people make up this Earth and no doubt there are other forms of civilisation out there we don't know about, so I am not alone in trying to help save this planet of people in my own conscience way; others are doing the same out there worldwide, and we are definitely evolving through a SUN-AGE ERA, and we are all going through a new awakening. Some people will feel this from their soul, some will be interested in exploring this new age and some will just ignore it all or laugh it off. I want to save my soul as it's the afterlife that matters more than my body, so good luck to those who don't believe what is happening in the cosmos and on Earth.

In my lifetime people have tried to mind control me, ostracise, ignore, shun me and be unhelpful, and I feel drained from living life, but I have re-energised myself knowing that we are evolving towards light. I believe I have evolved through four stages of life, and I am nearing the fifth stage. Sadly, I feel the fifth stage of life won't materialise till after death.

There are seven stages of life before you reach the higher dimension of energy, my intuition says these things. I just know these things instinctively.

My Aunty Frania said we all came from stars above – she told me that when I was nine years old as she was walking me home on a starry night. I think she knew that the planets and stars were all a part of our evolvement.

I do remember when I was seven years old, my mind told me that I was 358,000 in the queue before death, which worried me. I shivered and I promised God I would do my best to be loyal in my own way and listen and follow the right way with my gut instincts.

God extended my lifespan as I will be 58 in August this year (2019). Hopefully, I will live longer. **God willing.**

People and Giving 'Life'

People should treat others as they would like to be treated and spread love, peace and knowledge to everyone they meet and hopefully this grows as a chain reaction to have a fruitful karma and afterlife.

I have found this life very difficult to live through from the moment I breathed in my first breath, but I feel I have faced my challenges with great faith and strength, and I am grateful for the Polish family line I was born into.

I believe that if a life is aborted or miscarried that life rebirths elsewhere in someone else's body, and that's why if you are lucky in your life you might meet your soulmate or twin flame.

I thought that Peter was my soulmate, but I wasn't his, so he was an unsuitable opposite twin flame to my character and that's why we clashed. I felt his soul connection to me deeply, I sensed he was going to be a part of my life before even seeing him physically. Peter wrote a poem about being hurt in the womb, so why would he write that when he was born into a loving supportive family in the central west side of the counties? And I was born into the central east side, so it was impossible for us to meet earlier in life.

I believe that mothers have the ability to reject what they feel is unsuitable in their life – an extreme gut instinct to not keep a child must have a connection of unsuitability within.

This works the opposite way too: one of my sons had a problem within my womb and I was offered termination, but I wasn't enlightened to why I should terminate. My gut feeling told me that the problem was minor, and it turned out that a mark on the scan was no more than a lisp that my son outgrew.

It is unsettling how many mothers could have terminated a child based on a lisp.

When a responsibility of a conception happens, it is the responsibility of a mother to do what's best for herself.

I mentioned at the beginning of this book I knew what it felt like to be in the womb, so this shows how the sanctity of life is sacred. I am not a prophet, but I am an exceptionally highly stimulated woman capable of deep inner awareness, that I haven't fully explored as a person in my lifetime.

My Vision for the Future

I am tired of running away from man. I feel as if my body and mind are at war with each other, and that's why I am a reckless tornado at times. I believe there are negative energy forces getting in the way of people living a calm life.

When the world stands united

"as one positive frame of goodness"

the evil of the world will diminish like the Bible says, and therefore it's never happened. Not every human being will stand positively good in mind at the same time because of the complications of living in a changing multicultural world with individual rules, disciplines, living and working lives. Plus, the other side of the world sleeps and time keeps differently. But we *can* do good to raise our own well-being vibrations in our own personal space. When I re-read this *Petal* book, electric waves come out of my head and curl my hair, and that's where the saying "your hair curls" comes from, but usually it's in a shock form, not writing a book, so 'mind thought' played its part in creating electricity.

Naturally high people can create their own electricity.

I used to upset the black and white telly every time I moved, creating lines on it, and fuzzes and buzzes. I still do with the radio when high.

People must raise their energy with love, care and a positive attitude for the Earth to be a kinder planet, and for their soul to fly. People who are greedy and uncaring will succumb to the Earth as dust, but their genetic footprint will imprint in Earth's materials – this is where images of people and animals come from, even animals have unnecessary aggression.

Earth is volatile and very fragile and will be destroyed by natural disasters caused by man-made machinery and chemical errors and ruined by pollutions and lack of care *if things don't improve and change.*

I also believe the inner strength of women worldwide is becoming more powerful, and hopefully womanhood will win the war of men's turmoiled fighting minds and create a future civilisation of more peace and harmony.

People are getting tired of the sadness in the world and it is up to the spiritually connected humans, angels, creative people, and people with intuitive psychic abilities to sort this world, so our future generations have an Earth to cherish, and a life of fruitful fulfilment without negative baggage.

Mental Ill Health

Mental ill health is the biggest contribution to chaos, disorganisation, death and trauma to all living things and beauty. A dysfunctional mind is a danger to all and receives the least research, financial support, and understanding worldwide. Mental illness is misunderstood, because no one can see it, and mind function is the responsibility of the individual person. People fear the unstable and have no idea how to handle it.

Sadly, we are governed by chemical drugs because natural healing methods, which are far more beneficial to heal many physical and mental issues, are expensive to produce, and expensive to buy in retail too but not profitable for the chemical companies who rule people's health because the profits they gain are enormous from man-made chemicals.

The way forward is to educate those who don't understand mental ill health so a support network for the mentally ill grows to teach self-awareness. Anyone at any stage of their life can suffer mental health issues, even young children, so the eternal circle of mental ill health in family lines needs to be broken.

I will continue to work at fighting my bipolar conscious and raising self-awareness through writing.

I am hoping parents who suffer from mental health problems do not want their children or future generations to suffer too, so I will continue to voice my concerns in print, by addressing issues in a creative way to provide a better understanding of each other and the world problems we experience. I am deeply concerned that madness will spread in abundance with wrath worldwide, and confused minds will escalate to a mind world war that will go out of control like my mother prophesised.

My personal experience of mental madness and psychotic behaviour in my lifetime has given me the spirited passion to write all I witness, in the hope that others will get a grip of their own lives, or help a suffering member of family, and find a way to heal by bringing out their inner strength to be fruitful, positive and functional in kindness and faith.

Writing a book of experiences does help!

My three friends who I care for deeply have ridden the wave of my bipolar discontent, and my immediate family have watched me suffer the turmoil of an unstable mind. I am a benevolent, altruistic nice person in my soul, who absorbs the negativity of life. I am a force to be reckoned with, and I can bring the best out of people too and let them feel my love.

I hope the future is brighter for mental health issues and more people take an interest in studying the complex mind and seek jobs to benefit unsettled minds in the world. I hope mentally ill people see the light within them and get out of the bubble of oblivion and torment.

Stay strong. Stay focused. Keep busy. Channel energy.
BE POSITIVE STAY IN CONTROL

Bipolar Torments Of A Cold Winter

I saw his footprints in the whispering snow,
tired, tormented, stepping away,
away from my door, away from my heart,
and twelve hours later, the snow covered his
existence.
He was non-existent to me, the wrath of my mad
moods made it so.
I let him go, a broken man shuffling in the snow.
I drove him off with my winter rage, brought on by
a reaction, a lack of warmth and light.
The cold, fires an aggressive mouth, and words
are foul that make my mind scream, wailing like a
banshee waiting for death, or a kill.
I am thoughtless, I am full of regret, and my mind
is condensed like the snow packed into the path,
until it melts away.
Oh! for the Spring! to lift my mood, and to make
me smile and shine happiness,
from within, for a while
I saw his footprints in the snow, and wish the
winter mood not let him go.
I wanted him to stay, to keep my heart aglow,
but sadly, it's not to be, he chose to leave.
My heart lonely, once more, as the cold winds
blow. This sad bipolar woman can be
as cold as the ice packed snow.

KATE and the MOODS OF FLOWERS

The Flowers

Gorgeous flowers, blooms of wonder,
many moods of changes are seen.
Hues of colours, and scented smells,
exploding mixed emotions in a vase, with green coloured mottled leaves.
Soaked stems, and sugar gelled,
rainbow arrays of flowering beauty,
draw in buzzing bees to
pollinate naturally.
A petal can come from a rose,
all lush with romance,
and a drooping lily, saddened,
too tired to dance.
Daffodils standing to attention, and highly sprung, and sometimes
looking forlorn, and stooped humdrum.
Kate (Petal)
Kate can be wild, like the Heathers on a hill,
rocky and hard, she can cut a 'person's will.'
Kate's moods can be all flowers combined,
showering a charismatic affect, bubbly and blooming,
then she falls and becomes deathly low, a nervous wreck, and
unassuming.
The flowers eventually die, shrivelled and gone.
The petals dried and withered and not so strong,
but the changing moods and face, of Kate, lingers on, long after the
flowers have faded and gone.

PLANETS

I believe we are all matter from planets and stars, and I believe in aliens long existing before we evolved in our present human form. I believe that bipolar people come from planets that put out magnetic fields of great energy waves.

Jupiter has a massive aura of energy waves and it gives out the colourful aurora borealis – better known as the Northern Lights. I saw a poster of Jupiter in a gallery shop, and my heart warmed so much, and I felt close to the planet. I bought a similar poster on line which now hangs on my wall.

I love colour, I love decorating envelopes when sending post, even payment bills. I am very creative in arts and crafts, and I believe my energy waves stem from Jupiter.

Saturn is also a strong magnetic energy field and all these connections of planets have fascinated people since ancient times. I also feel that I will meet Greek Zeus known as Jupiter in another life dimension of time. The fear of lightning is close to my soul, so there must be something special about the eternal God of lightning, thunder and sky.

I gained excellent learning ability in high school:

96 % assessment pass in classical studies and 92% in Latin as a young school pupil; so for someone born in England to Polish parents my knowledge and understanding of those periods were exceptional.

Solid and liquid matter and gases were around before the formation of living human and animal life and therefore we originated as part of science and nature.

Our existence in the beginning was particles of matter, formed with 11 elements that help to create our body, which is nature. Science and nature go hand in hand and thus we must realise that God is science and nature too, but overall an energy force that revolves our universe, bonding us through a pattern of energy airwaves.

I quite often feel that I am being pushed out of this world, but I hang on in because of the strength of my will and the power of my inner energy.

Great creative intelligent people have walked this Earth since time began; they are still watching over us somehow. Sadly, the intelligence in people that has shaped our world today in the second decade of the 21st century, is now destroying the planet, with a fast life burn.

It is time to heal the planet.

Not tomorrow. Today. Now.
We have 30 years to heal this planet and steer the inhabitants and animal kingdom to a healthier living environment. Thereafter...
What will be.
Will be.
The course of the future will have no return. Heaven or hell?
Both are on this Earth!
I hope the future will be heavenly for all eternally who are born. Whether it's just their lifetime of living in a body or by afterlife's conscious soul. Let's hope we have a protected fruitful Earth to live happily in forever more.

I hope and live in faith this will happen, but it's not likely to happen in my lifetime as a human.

Wouldn't it be great if people could explore the universe like Star Trek films? Then return to their own motherland they were born into;

Our precious Earth! And not have to find a new

Planet to inhabit.

CONCLUSION

My favourite moral-guiding books and films of all time are C.S. Lewis' famous stories about *Narnia.*

The Lion, The Witch and The Wardrobe, a story about a lion called Aslan and four children who find a magical mystery wonderland through a wardrobe door. The story is a wonderful example of how good triumphs over evil, and how kindness saves a life, let alone the day.

C.S. Lewis is thought to have based each of the Narnia Chronicles on planets in the solar system as he was thought to have been a fanatical astrologist. The book was widely discussed – whether Narnia was based on Christ and Christian morals, or Islam, or both. After I read the book at the age of 11, I dreamt one night when 12 years old, that a large lion came into my room; I opened my eyes and a lion's head stared at me in the darkness. Then disappeared.

I believe that Aslan represents all great prophets that have bestowed their knowledge of God. I believe that God showed himself to me as a lion's head.

God also showed himself to me, as a ball of orange glow, four years ago, while I was praying.

The Narnia film is very spiritual but at the same time very cosmic too. God is both spiritual and cosmic.

I felt every vibe the Narnia story put out and C.S. Lewis was my favourite author in my teenage years. Kindness in soul, and a strong controlled will, wins over evil and destruction. The wicked never win wars or we wouldn't be here to continue to live and procreate and evolve further.

C.S. Lewis Quotes

"You don't have a Soul. You *are* a Soul.
You have a Body."

"You are never too old to set another goal
or dream a new dream."

Soul Within

The seat of the soul is the pineal gland. A man's soul energy comes from the centre of their head, which is close to the seventh chakra (crown). This is known as the *Eye of God*. A woman's soul energy lies in the navel area at the solar plexus, the *Lustrous Gem*, the third chakra. The woman's soul lies in the part of the stomach where the umbilical cord attaches behind the belly button, for she is the giver of creating potential life. A woman's soul energy from the umbilical cord will help to push the birth of a baby in labour.

The soul detaches itself from the body after death through the pineal gland. If we consciously exercise a higher dimension of living, we move on more freely after death. That's why practising yoga, or other forms of meditational healing, helps, together with a healthier lifestyle, to feed the mind and body, like exercising and absorbing healing aromatherapy and various forms of herbs and spices.

Everything you read in books is written out of knowledge of knowing so never knock someone's written word – they know what they say. Men and women develop their motivation, purpose and confidence differently as humans, men mainly through mind thoughts and women through gut reactions. But as we are made up of different quantities of male and female hormones, people can experience their soul motivation in either of the ways. This is what makes humans interesting and different and versatile – because we are made up of both sexes. We can be productive and non-productive, strong-willed or weak-willed, lucky and unlucky.

The soul is protected within the Chakras.

The Chakras are forms of energy that circulate throughout the whole of our body and create a barrier outside too. This is how we develop an aura.

I recommend this website as an interesting place to explore energy points:

http://www. crystalinks. com/chakra2

Journey

Our lifespan is a journey that is mapped out according to thought processes and physical make-up from birth. We can change thought pattern as humans if we want to.

We are the drivers of our own destiny and we have choices in the routes of life we create. Life is challenging and some adventures in our lifetime are unavoidable. There are evil forces of extreme negativity that try to damage survival, but it is up to the individual to tackle these obstacles and follow their instinct. Darkness must never guide you, so learn to shine your light within, outwards, to have a happy, stable life, of positive outlook and well-being.

NEVER WEAR FEAR. BE STRONG.

Blessings, love and light to all.

Kate Dobrowolska

Earth

Do people care about the Earth?
The way things are?
When they drive a van, a lorry or a car?
When they travel on a train, or by plane,
to go to work or for a holiday?
I take a deep breath and
look up to the sky,
I watch a bird flying high.
I walk through wet grass,
I see daisies sway,
In the cool wind today.
I hug a tree giving me the air
That I breathe. This matters to me.
The air is a passage of time,
unseen waves as people walk by.
I feel the Earth move under my foot,
the soil is sinking and shifting tree roots.
I wonder what is to come?
Are we all doomed? and done?
The wind blows a gust,
the ground shakes,
the dust kicks up,
a tree branch breaks.
Leaves all scatter and
the crows start to caw,
the sky goes smoky
as the rain starts to fall.
Pollution rises when the sun comes out
the clouds pink and purple.

What is that all about?
Is this what we breathe into our lungs?
Poisons from places that are
killing someone?
The Earth is our life source,
helping people to survive,
so why are people neglecting it
by the modern way of life?

The Matrix

We are all living in the Matrix, governed by procedures, structures, conformity. Time was developed by clock form, but who is to say what is real? What is past? What is present? What is the future?

Or what is today or tomorrow?

Strip this away and we live in a disillusioned world, that causes a lot of chaos.

The only way to escape this cocooned orderly life is to be at one with yourself, to look after your mind, body and soul.

To slow down your pace of life, and lower the needs of materialism which is useless when your soul moves on.

When we breathe life and take the last breath in death as humans, our soul will live on, so the most important thing to nourish is your soul and raise your self-awareness, your senses, and embrace a spiritual awakening more fulfilling than living life as humans.

After all, you can achieve a lot in body form, but you will achieve more in the afterlife if you reach for the light as one.

"YOU ARE ENOUGH."

Peace, love, light, hope, faith, belief,
Friendship, support, care,
Please encourage a better world out there.
For the sake of the future
Generations of children.

Live life
Enjoy life
Be kind, joyful, positive
and benevolent towards others.

Kate x